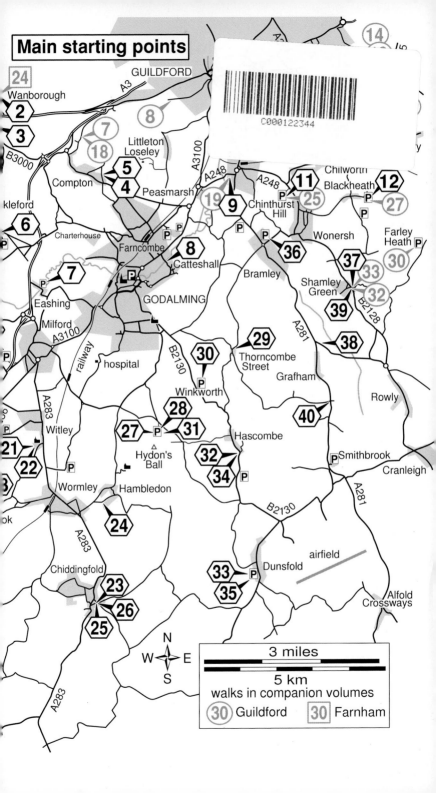

Main starting points

C000122344

1 Puttenham Common to the Hog's Back

About 7 km/4¼ miles with an extension of 1 km/¾ mile; hilly; good in winter; soft sand in summer. The Common is confusing and best comprehended in small doses. If new to Puttenham Common start along the east boundary, ①.
To extend over part of the Common, start at ⓔ but allow time for confusion.
OS maps 1:25000 145 Guildford, 1:50000 186 Aldershot.

Start at Puttenham Common Top car park, SU 920 461, or Puttenham village (roadside parking), SU 930 478.

Linking walks   2❖   3◈   6✳   13✦
   21 ✳   22 ✳   24 ❖

The Good Intent ☎ 01483 810387
Jolly Farmer Harvester ☎ 01483 810374

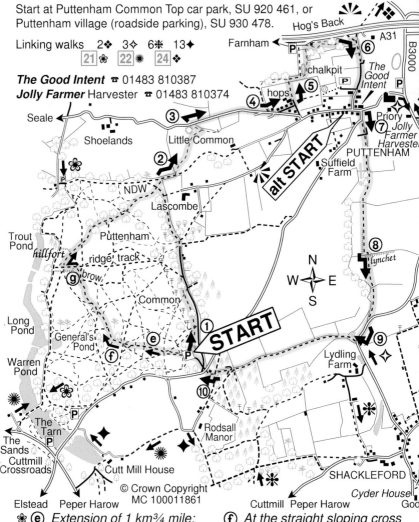

© Crown Copyright
MC 100011861

✿ ⓔ *Extension of 1 km/¾ mile:*
At the corner diagonally opposite the car park entrance drop down the steep path (100m). Don't join the valley path but cross the slight rise and keep on, forking R when the path splits near the end (300m).

ⓕ *At the straight sloping cross path, stay ahead over a rise, down into the dip with several side paths (300m), up past a L fork (50m) and over the brow (200m) to the straight level ridge track across the* <u>heath</u> *on top (100m). Look back.*

2

⑩ *Turn L through the ramparts of the hillfort (a not very large bank) (100m) and take the first side path back R soon descending the hillside, over another downhill path (200m) and into a dip (100m). Disregarding side paths, continue ahead up to the converging path (150m). Follow this into the deep dip then up over the perimeter path (300m) and into the corner of the Common (80m).* ➔②

① Take the flat path at the corner of the car park away from the road, converging on the E boundary track of Puttenham Common. Continue on the track to the second house (700m). Stay ahead, past the side path R just after the house and the next side path R (350m) to the crosspath (80m) then turn R into the corner of the Common (70m).

② Bear R on the North Downs Way between fields (100m). At the end of the L field bear L on the side path undulating obliquely down through Little Common (in late summer obscured by bracken) (400m). At the next field turn down the path L to the road below (50m).

③ Follow the road R (600m).

④ After the 1st house L bear L on Dark Lane to the junction (150m).

⑤ Turn L to the farm sheds and go straight on up the middle of the hop field (150m). Climb the bank and turn R along the hillside (80m) then go up the L field boundary and through the trees to the Hog's Back car park (250m). Turn R. ❖

⑥ From the car park follow the road R towards Guildford either on the verge or in the trees (300m) to the footpath down R (30m before a drive). If traffic is light cross the dual carriageway from the drive to see the view then return. Descend the path, which becomes a track, then School Lane, to the village street in Puttenham (500m). Turn L to the **Good Intent** (50m). ✧

⑦ Opposite the pub, walk along Suffield Lane to the bend near the gate of Puttenham Priory (70m). Take the footpath ahead at the L edge of the field then between fields and on along above the bank (lynchet) in the next field (900m).

⑧ Just round the corner of the lynchet drop to the next field and go straight over to the exit hidden under the L brow of the dip (200m). Descend the short steep slope and go on round R to the road (250m).

⑨ Go down the road R (130m) ✳ and turn into the next field R. Follow the L edge (lynchet) round to the large field (150m) then keep on ahead at the R edge of the fields up the slight valley (700m). After the last field stay ahead through the trees and drop to the sunken bridleway (300m). ✦✳

⑩ Slightly L, go up the other side and past the garden to the road opposite Top car park (150m).

The Puttenham **hop field** is the only remaining one in Surrey. The variety is *Fuggles* grown for the Hog's Back Brewery and other real ale brewers. So far, it has not suffered verticillium wilt, a fungal disease that would end the cultivation. A few of the plants are male (1:500) and look different. The oast houses below the church, now residential, functioned until 1970 and the hops are now dried in the shed in the field. Hop growing came to the Farnham area just before 1600 and dominated agriculture on the malmstone in the 18th and 19th centuries.

2 Wanborough and the Hog's Back

About 7½ km/4½ miles; a scenic walk over fields and a vineyard, good all the year round; hilly, numerous stiles and two irksome road crossings on the Hog's Back. OS maps 1:25000 145 Guildford, 1:50000 186 Aldershot.

Start from Wanborough beside the Great Barn, SU 934 488.

Linking walks   1❖   3✳   4✪   ⑤✳   ⑦★   ⑱✳   23❖   24✿

Watts Gallery *Tea Shop* ☎ 01483 813590
Watts Gallery ☎ 01483 810235

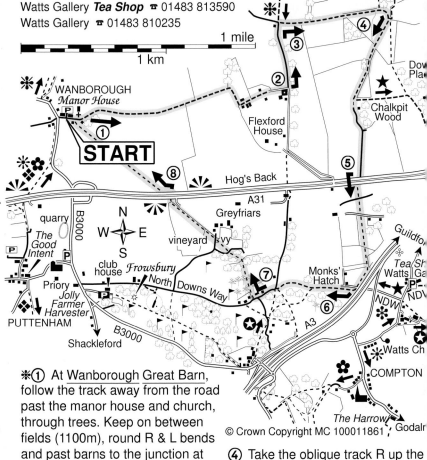

© Crown Copyright MC 100011861

✳① At <u>Wanborough</u> <u>Great Barn</u>, follow the track away from the road past the manor house and church, through trees. Keep on between fields (1100m), round R & L bends and past barns to the junction at the East Flexford houses (500m).

② Turn L down the cart track to the junction after the house (400m).

③ Go R on the bridleway under trees between fields and eventually into a field (450m). Follow the L edge and go round the end corner R of the wood to the path junction at the hedge bend (250m).

④ Take the oblique track R up the middle of the field to trees (200m) then along the L edge (300m). ★ Stay ahead to the side track at the corner of Chalkpit Wood. The public footpath is over the rough ground to the houses but walkers tend to keep to the edge of the field to the gate. Join the drive and ascend to the top of the <u>Hog's Back</u> (500m).

4

⑤ Cross the dual carriageway, turn R (30m) and take the path into the field. Go straight down, over a rack and a terrace then slightly L to the tarmac lane (200m). Stay ahead down the field parallel with the R fence then beside the bottom edge past a knoll with trees (300m), across the end of a narrow field and beside the embankment of the A3 to the drive and gateway of Monks' Hatch (200m). ❀✿❂✳

⑥ Now follow the North Downs Way R, joined by tracks R (600m) and L (150m) at the next group of houses. After this (30m) is the drive of Monks Grove Farm R. ❖

⑦ Turn R on the path beside the drive. Pass between the gardens and go straight up the slope, over the golf fairways with belts of trees then through the wood (300m). After the wood bear L on the path through scrub to the farm track (100m). Stay ahead obliquely across Greyfriars Vineyard (100m), the (private) car park and track into the next part of the vineyard. Keep on up the R edge to the top of the Hog's Back (400m).

⑧ Cross the dual carriageway then turn L (30m). Descend the footpath (old carriage road) to Wanborough church (800m). ✳

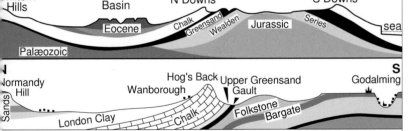

The Hog's Back is the most contorted part of the North Downs chalk ridge. The chalk was once continuous over the Weald but the middle has been eaten out by erosion to leave this broken edge; the South Downs are the other edge. To the north the chalk dips under the London Basin, re-emerging as the Chilterns.

The field track from Wanborough runs along the edge of the London Clay on which grow cereals. Water out of the chalk leaks over the edge of the clay as springs which were the likely cause of pre-historic settlement. The wooded hills visible to the north are the escarpment of the Tertiary (Bagshot) Sands plateau with infertile heath stretching to Bracknell. It resists erosion because of a cap of flint gravel washed out from the chalk dome by the early Ice Age torrents.

Melbourne Rock, a hard layer in the Middle Chalk, was quarried at Puttenham and used in the pillars of Compton Church. The Upper Greensand under the Chalk permits the hops to grow at Puttenham and yields the white malmstone of the houses in Seale. Gault clay accounts for the dry valley beneath the ridge as it allows the edge of the chalk to be undermined by erosion; it provided the raw material for the terracotta tiles of the Watts chapel. The Folkstone Beds, the top stratum of the Lower Greensand, are unlithified sands lacking calcium which cause the heath of Puttenham golf course and Common. The calcareous Bargate sandstone forms the plateau above Compton stretching southwards to Hascombe with wheatfields and disused quarries for the brown building stone.

3 Puttenham and Shackleford

About 9 km/5½ miles with a bluebell extension of 1¼ km/¾ miles through Compton; good throughout the year; farmland and golf courses with long views; one short steep hill; one nasty road crossing and the hazards of golf.
OS maps 1:25000 145 Guildford, 1:50000 186 Aldershot.

Start from the large layby, SU 934 479, on the B3000 at the Puttenham side road or from Shackleford car park, SU 935 453, in the road fork.

Linking walks   1✧   2✳   4✿   5✿   ⑱✿   23✳   24✳

Jolly Farmer (Harvester) ☎ 01483 810374
The Cyder House ☎ 01483 810360
The Good Intent ☎ 01483 810387
The Harrow Inn ☎ 01483 810594
The Squirrel Inn ☎ 01483 860223

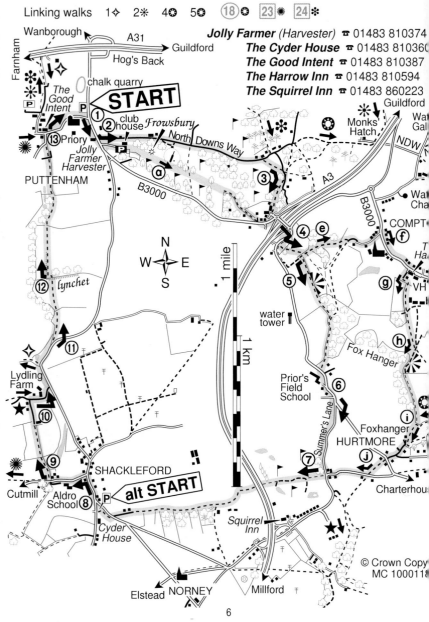

6

① Walk down the B3000 to the **Jolly Farmer** *(Harvester)* (100m) then cross the road to the side track L (North Downs Way).

ⓐ *Alternative: Follow way marks along the golf course (1200m) and turn L along the road (150m).* ➔④

② Follow the NDW past Clear Barn (400m) and a side track L (300m), to houses L (500m). ◉

③ Opposite the 2nd cottage take the path R obliquely over the golf course into the wood, disregarding golf tracks (150m). On the vehicle track turn R to the first house (50m) then fork R to the next buildings (300m). Turn L up to the road.

④ Cross the A3 bridge (150m) and go R (Charterhouse) (150m). At the bend, opposite the first drive, go L up the fields to the cross path under the trees on top (250m).

ⓔ *Extension of 1¼ km/¾ mile via Compton: Turn L down the path and continue along the lane to the village street in Compton (600m).*

ⓕ *Follow the pavements down R to the **Harrow** (300m).*

ⓖ *Turn R on the drive beside the pub (70m) and L behind gardens (50m) then go up the R edge of the field over the rise (200m) and straight across the next field in the same line to the cart track (200m).*

ⓗ *Follow it up R over the spur of the hill and down to the corner (200m) and continue up round the top edge of the next field (300m).*

ⓘ *Just before the next corner, exit R and take the uphill path (150m). Stay ahead on the track, (150m), over the main road and along the track opposite (150m).* ★

ⓙ *Turn R on the road to the bend at Summer's Lane (300m).* ➔⑦

⑤ Enter the flat field above the hillside and follow the onward path at the L edge (above the Bargate escarpment) past a water tower far R (350m) to the road opposite Prior's Field School (450m).

⑥ Walk along the road L (250m) then R down Summer's Lane to the road junction (500m). ★

⑦ Take the path R across the golf course in a straight line: faint path then vehicle track then faint path, to the A3 (500m). Cross the dual carriageway. Stay ahead on the path, round a L bend (100m), past a side path (250m) to the road (700m). Cross the road to the path up the bank and go R to the road junction (150m). (**Cyder House** L).

⑧ From the car park walk through Shackleford (200m) and take Cutmill side road L to the end of the houses R (250m). ✳

⑨ Go R along the bottom edge of the fields. Stay ahead past houses to the wall of Lydling Farm (550m).

⑩ Go R on the drive past the farm and down to the pond then L up the road. Disregard the path L at the next bend ✧ (150m) but join the path in the next field L (150m).

⑪ Follow the L edge of the field up the short steep slope under trees into the next field (250m). Over the brow bear slightly R and climb the bank (lynchet) into the next field (200m).

⑫ Go round the corner and on along the edge. Stay ahead to Puttenham (Puttenham Priory far R) (900m) and along Suffield Lane to the **Good Intent** (70m). ✳✳

⑬ Turn R up the road past the church (converted oast houses L) to the main road and layby (400m).

4 Compton and Binscombe

About 8½ km/5¼ miles; good all the year round; mainly farming country; bluebell woods. OS maps 1:25000 145 Guildford, 1:50000 186 Aldershot.

Start from the roadside opposite the *Withies* at Compton, SU 963 468, or outside the Watts Gallery or Watts Chapel.

Linking walks   2✪   3✪   5✻   6✿   ⑦✷   ⑱✿   24✿

The Harrow Inn ☎ 01483 810594   **The Withies** ☎ 01483 421158
Watts Gallery *Tea Shop* ☎ 01483 813590   Watts Gallery ☎ 01483 810235

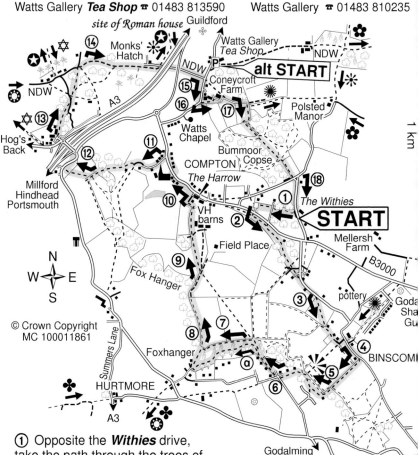

① Opposite the **Withies** drive, take the path through the trees of Compton Common. Follow it past the first house to the 2nd (300m).

② Turn L to the road and cross to the tarmac path behind the trees (50m). Turn L and follow it round to the next road (500m). Carry on along the road round the L bend to the 2nd field (200m).

③ Cross the field to the top L corner (200m). Carry on L along the path behind the houses (150m).

④ At the end turn L (50m) into Binscombe. Follow the road R past the Quakers' burial ground and on (150m) then walk up the R edge of the next field R to the top (300m).

⑤ Take the path round the top of the adjacent field R either in the field or through the trees above it (250m). Watch out for an upward path L, 50m before the next corner. Climb the stepped path (up the Bargate escarpment) to the flat top and pass between gardens (200m).

⑥ At the road bend, turn R along another path between gardens and keep on to the edge of the escarpment (300m).

ⓐ *Bluebell alternative 200m more: Diverge L on the path up through the coppice above the escarpment to the end (500m) and double back down the path below the house into the field (200m)* ➔⑧

⑦ Stay ahead to the stepped path and descend (100m). Turn L up the path between the escarpment and the field (350m). ❂❀ After the R bend (20m) enter the field R.

⑧ Follow the path L round the top edge of the field (300m). Carry on up the curving track in the 2nd field to the top of the rise (100m) then start descending towards the large house, Field Place (100m).

⑨ Halfway down enter the field L and cross obliquely to the L of the distant barns (200m). In the next field follow the L edge over the rise and down past the barns (200m). Turn L behind the garden (50m) and R to the **Harrow** (70m).

⑩ Walk up the village street through Compton, past White Hart Cottage and Eastbury Manor. Visit the church then carry on up the pavement opposite, watching out for Eastbury Lane L (300m).

⑪ Follow the lane (250m) and fork R up the hill path. Look for the stile to the field R on the brow (350m).

⑫ Cross down through the middle of two fields to the road (200m). Follow the pavement down R and over the A3 bridge (300m). ✿

⑬ Continue ahead to the garage (50m) then take the path R into the wood. ❂ Stay ahead, over the cart track obliquely, near houses R (300m), to the 4-way junction at the North Downs Way (250m).

⑭ Turn R along the NDW and stay on it to the Monks' Hatch bridges (600m).✳ Follow the tarmac NDW under the bridges to the road (400m). ❀ (Watts Gallery & **Tea Shop** are L 100m).

⑮ Follow the road R to the end of the Coneycroft Farm buildings (200m). *If visiting* Watts Chapel *carry on along the lane (200m) and into the cemetery then return.*

⑯ Take the path back L zigzagging beside the barns and continue on the straight farm track (400m). ✳

⑰ At the end fence, turn R on the path which skirts the field into the wood (200m) then keep to the main path to Polsted Lane (500m).

⑱ Slightly L (10m) continue on the road ahead to the **Withies** (200m).

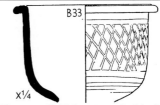

Romano-British pot, probably 2nd century, found with many other shards when the Binscombe Crescent houses were built in 1953. The site is thought to have been an ordinary homestead rather than a villa. The archæologist's sketch shows the section as well as surface. SAC 57 1960 *Romano-British Farms*

5 Binscombe and Loseley

About 8 km/5 miles with an extension of 1 km/¾ mile to Watts Gallery; farm country and bluebell woods. In summer Loseley House can be visited *en route*. OS maps 1:25000 145 Guildford, 1:50000 186 Aldershot.

Start from Compton. Park at the roadside opposite *The Withies*, SU 963 468.

Linking walks 3❂ 4✳ ⑦❖ ⑱✳ ⑲❖ ㉔✳

The Withies ☎ 01483 421158   **The Harrow Inn** ☎ 01483 8103594
Watts Gallery **Tea Shop** ☎ 01483 8133590   Watts Gallery ☎ 01483 810235
Loseley House ☎ 01483 304440

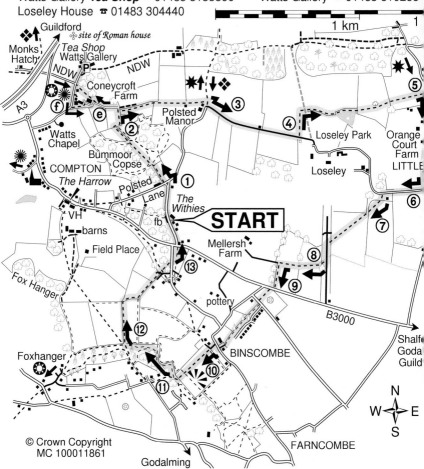

© Crown Copyright
MC 100011861

① From the **Withies** walk along the lane away from the main road to the junction with Polsted Lane (200m). Slightly L take the path into the trees. Disregard all side paths. At the end of the wood (500m) skirt round the R edge of the fields to

the path R just before the concrete farm track (200m). ❖

ⓔ *Extension of 1 km/¾ mile to Watts Gallery: Go L on the concrete farm track (200m), R on the footpath at the start of the buildings (150m) and R on the road (100m).*

10

Return along the road to the end of the farm buildings L (200m).

f *Turn L on the path which zigzags beside the barns. Keep on to the end of the farm track (400m).*

② Follow the footpath outside the fence of the hillside field, ultimately past a garden R and down into the deep sunken track (600m). ✳

③ Turn R down to the lane near Polsted Manor (30m) and L up the track that continues from the lane. Keep on past a house L (400m) to the Loseley Park gateway (300m).

④ Take the footpath L along the boundary (200m). The path bends R along the bottom edge of the fields, crosses a farm track and passes the pond (400m). Loseley House is visible far R. Keep on over the fields, rising slightly L, and go out to the road at Pillarbox Cottage in Littleton (500m).✧

⑤ Go R on the road down through the village and over a rise (600m).

⑥ Turn R on the tarmac Loseley drive to the first house L (300m).

⑦ Next to the house turn L on the track into the field (50m). Cross the R corner (100m). Continue through the next field in the same oblique line to exit between the gateway and the bottom corner (400m).

⑧ Outside the field follow another Loseley Drive L over the culvert (80m). Turn R along the stream to the field and and follow the R edge. When the stream bends R stay ahead to the next hedge (350m).

⑨ Turn L along the hedge to the road (200m). 30m R, cross into the football field opposite and go over it parallel with the R end (100m). Cross the next road to the grass, slightly L, and follow the path R of the side road under trees and on to Binscombe (450m).

⑩ On the road turn R past the Quakers' cemetery (40m) then L on the track between the houses (50m). When it bends, go straight on up the field (300m). Look back.

The Hog's Back is the hill L. Beyond the cluster of radio masts is Guildford at the notch where the River Wey cuts the chalk ridge. At the highest point Semaphore House gleams in the sun. The North Downs disappear behind Chantries Hill with St Martha's as the bump on the R end. The sharp green spire in front of Chantries is Shalford Church. The river runs between it and the Mount Browne Surrey Police HQ at the lone radio mast slightly L. The large house just beyond Binscombe is Loseley. The distant eminence R is the Leith Hill range. The closer Farley Hill and the plateau behind you are capped by Bargate sandstone and form the portals of the Wey gorge.

---

⑪ Continue up into the trees on the escarpment. Just round the bend (20m) branch R on the small winding path near the bottom edge of the wood (250m). At the gulley descend briefly (40m) then climb the L bank. Disregard paths in the fields below and keep on to the end of the wood at the path junction below steps (200m). ✳⬡

⑫ Go down the path between fields (300m). Cross into the field below and turn R. Follow the R edges round down to the end of the fields (300m). Stay ahead over cross tracks through the trees, converging on the road (100m).

⑬ Cross to the grass and turn L parallel with the road (100m). Keep on over the main road along the lane to the *Withies* (200m).

6 Shackleford, Eashing and Peper Harow

About 8 km/5 miles, with extensions of 400m/¼ mile and ¾ km/½ mile; fields and woods with a dash across the A3; soft sand and nettles in summer, little shade, gentle rises. OS maps 1:25000 145 Guildford, 1:50000 186 Aldershot.

Start from Shackleford car park in the road fork, SU 935 453, or from the little car park in Lower Eashing at the west end of the bridges, SU 946 438.

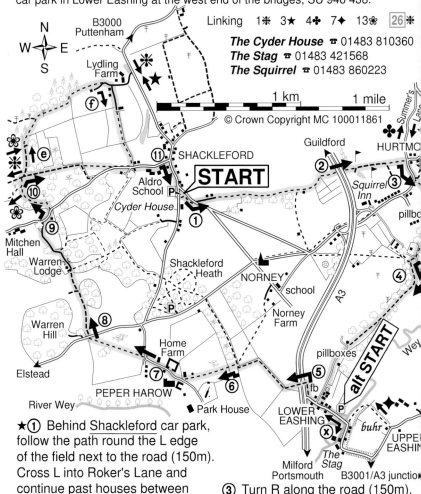

Linking 1❋ 3★ 4♣ 7✦ 13❀ 26 ❋

The Cyder House ☎ 01483 810360
The Stag ☎ 01483 421568
The Squirrel ☎ 01483 860223

1 km   1 mile

© Crown Copyright MC 100011861

★① Behind Shackleford car park, follow the path round the L edge of the field next to the road (150m). Cross L into Roker's Lane and continue past houses between fields and trees, bending L & R near the end, to the A3 (1100m).

② Cross the dual carriageway and keep on in the same line straight across the golf course: on grass then cart track until it bends, then grass to the houses. Exit at a road bend in Hurtmore (500m). ♣

③ Turn R along the road (150m). When it curves R, bear L down the footpath next to a drive. Disregard the uphill side paths and continue down to a drive and garden wall in the Wey gorge (600m). ✦

④ Go R a few paces on the drive then turn off L, up the bridleway on the valleyside. Disregard the path

12

R up into the trees. Continue on the level bridleway to the pillboxes then on the concrete farm track into Lower Eashing (1200m).

Ⓧ *Extension of 400 km/¼ mile into Eashing: Go L to Eashing Bridges (250m) and round the bend as far as **The Stag** (150m), then return.*

⑤ Walk out of the village to the A3 (100m). Turn R up over the bridleway bridge to the field (150m) and follow the R edge round to the trees at the second corner (500m).

⑥ Join the track out of the field but immediately turn L through the trees (40m). In the next field go straight on parallel with the bottom edge. Park House is visible L beyond the cricket field. Pass L of the dovecote and barn to the church at Peper Harow (350m).

⑦ From the church walk up the lane (50m). Step into the yard R to see Home Farm then carry on up the lane (250m). When it bends R, go on into the field and straight up to the far top corner (400m).

⑧ Cross the road into the field. Follow the track to Warren Lodge (450m). Disregard the footpath R and go straight on (450m).

⑨ At the road go R (100m). At the R bend turn L up the winding path into the wood round the end of the field (300m). ❀ Keep on up to the 4-way junction (70m). ✳

ⓔ *Extension of ¾ km/½ mile: Take the track ahead, between the wood and fields all the way to Lydling Farm house L (1100m).*

ⓕ *Backtrack (30m) and take the side turn past Lydling Cottages to the end (150m). Carry straight on to the bottom of the fields and join the road (400m). Turn L into Shackleford (250m).* ➔⑪

⑩ Take the track R through the wood to the bend (400m) then go down the field ahead converging on the R edge to the bend halfway down (200m). Drop to the road and carry on into Shackleford (400m).

⑪ Turn R to the car park (200m). The **Cyder House** is R (100m).

Charterhouse School has spires which make it a distinctive landmark on many of the walks in this book though there is no public path or road which allows a close view. It is one of the best known public schools, with 700 boys and 6th form girls. The name derives from its original site near Barts in London where a Carthusian monastery had stood. Thomas Sutton bought the post-Dissolution property from the Duke of Norfolk in 1611 and founded the school. It removed to Godalming when the main building was completed in 1872. *Photo Adrian Furniss*

7 Eashing, the Wey Gorge and Godalming

About 8 km/5 miles with a short cut of 1¾ km/1 mile bypassing Godalming town centre; good views in winter, few stiles, one steep slope, quite a lot of tarmac. OS maps 1:25000 145 Guildford, 1:50000 186 Aldershot.

Start at Lower Eashing, from the little car park at the west end of the bridges, SU 946 438. If parking at Godalming, use in the long layby in Borough Road.

Linking walks   6✦ 8❋

The King's Arms ☎ 0845 805 3478
The Red Lion ☎ 011483 423428
The Stag ☎ 01483 421568
The Squirrel ☎ 01483 860223

© Crown Copyright
MC 100011861

✦① From Eashing bridges walk through the village towards the A3 (200m). Turn R on the tarmac drive before the last house and keep on along the concrete farm track (400m). After pillboxes stay ahead on the bridleway round L into a side valley where a drive and bridleway join L on two sides of the garden wall (900m).

ⓐ *Alternative: In winter try taking the higher path. Go L on the bridleway after the wall (60m) then R up the valley side (100m). Near the top turn R on the path along the steep side of the gorge (800m). Butcher's Broom abounds.*

ⓑ *After turning into the next side valley, go down the stepped side path R then out down the tarmac drive of Charterhouse and over Peperharow Road (250m) to the footpath opposite.* ✦③

② Follow the drive round the end of the valley and stay ahead L of the house through the Wey gorge to Peperharow Road in Godalming (800m).

③ Walk down the path beside the houses to the river (100m) then L along the bank (450m). Join the tarmac path and stay on it over the drive of Westbrook Mill to Borough Road (700m). Turn R under the (Portsmouth-Waterloo) railway then, behind the wall R, follow the footpath over the river (200m).

Ⓢ *Short cut of 1¾ km/1 mile: Turn R along Vicarage Walk and cross the River Ock (100m). Follow the lane R under the railway and up past Westbrook House to the top (600m). At the L bend continue ahead on the drive past Shepherd Cottage (public footpath)(80m).* ✦⑩

14

④ Cross the road into the park. Go past the <u>Phillips Memorial</u> cloisters and follow the riverside path (opposite the <u>Lammas Land</u>) to the next road (700m). ✳

⑤ Over the road and river, turn back R around the wall. Follow the river bank to the L bend opposite Godalming Wharf at the end of the <u>Godalming Navigation</u> (300m). Return to the bridge and cross it.

⑥ Walk up Bridge Street (300m). Bear R past the ***King's Arms*** and go on along High Street (350m).

⑦ After the Pepper-pot (50m) go R on the passageway next to the ***Red Lion***, over the road, down Mill Lane to Hatch Mill on the River Ock and up to the railway (350m).

⑧ Pass under the station to the drive parallel with the railway and turn L to the houses (300m).

⑨ Go up round the bend in the drive and continue up the path under trees to the farm on top (400m). Carry on along the drive (or the edge of the R field) round the ½R bend to the sharp L bend near the cottage (200m).

⑩ Follow the level tarmac drive between flat fields above the Ock and Wey gorges (Charterhouse spires back R) to the road (900m).

⑪ Go R beside the road (250m), round the L bend at Upper Eashing and on (250m).

⑫ At the first house R turn into the field and go straight along the shoulder (edge of the burh) to the end (250m). Descend L through the trees on the river bank to Eashing Bridges near the cliff (200m). The ***Stag*** is ahead, beyond the site of <u>Eashing Mill</u> (offices) (100m).

Charterhouse Hog's Back
Puttenham
A3/B3000 junction
(b)
Peperharow Road
③
alt START
railway
Wey Gorge
Guildford
Westbrook mill
Lammas Land ⑤
S
underpass
⑧
④ King's Arms wharf
Star
P Sun
mill P
High Street B2130
⑨ ⑦ Red Lion
River Ock
A3100 GODALMING
Holloway Hill Winkworth
Tuesley Hascombe
ford mill Tuesley

Escingum **burh** is recorded in the "Burhal Hidage", written around 915. Burhs became boroughs. They were 27 barracks set up in Wessex to counter Viking predations. Probably initiated by Alfred the Great, they provided mobilization depots, refuges and strong points for militias to drive the Danes out of Wessex. For manning and sustenance they were apportioned parts of the kingdom. The 600 hides allocated to Escingum indicate a garrison of 600 men. Four men were stipulated for each pole (5½ yards) of wall. These figures accord with the rectangle of land at Eashing between the river cliff and two dry side valleys (where the road and footpath lie) if the cliff was unmanned. The nearest burhs were at Southwark, Winchester, Chichester and Sashes Island on the Thames at Cookham. Why Eshing lost its importance is obscure but many burhs became new towns as the influx of defenders required markets and services. More burhs were added in Mercia when the non-Danish parts were absorbed by Edward the Elder, Alfred's son, and they were copied by the Franks.

8 Catteshall and Unsted

About 7½ km/4½ miles with an extension of 3 km/2 miles. Best when the Navigation is active; hilly; soft sand on the towpath in summer, boggy in wet seasons in ⓘ. OS maps 1:25000 145 Guildford, 1:50000 186 Aldershot.

Start from the kerbside on Catteshall Bridge, SU 981 445. On the extension use the car park at the east end of Broad Water, SU 985 453.

Linking walks 7✳ 9✳ 29☆

Hector's on the Wey at Farncombe Boat House ☎ 01483 418769
The Manor Inn ☎ 01483 427134   **The Leathern Bottle** ☎ 01483 425642

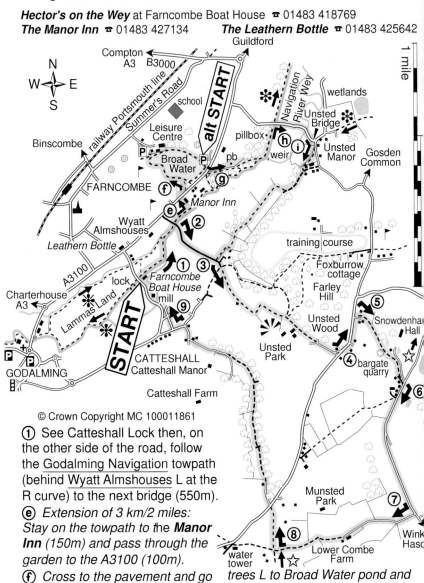

© Crown Copyright MC 100011861

① See Catteshall Lock then, on the other side of the road, follow the Godalming Navigation towpath (behind Wyatt Almshouses L at the R curve) to the next bridge (550m).

ⓔ *Extension of 3 km/2 miles: Stay on the towpath to the* **Manor Inn** *(150m) and pass through the garden to the A3100 (100m).*

ⓕ *Cross to the pavement and go R (100m). Find a path through the*

trees L to Broad Water pond and walk round the pond clockwise to

16

the car park at the corner back near the A3100 (700m).

(g) *From the corner of the pond cross the road, just before the outflow, to the gate (50m) then follow the footpath R of the fence to the Navigation opposite a weir (400m). Turn L along the towpath to the road bridge (250m).* ✳

(h) *Follow the road over the Wey Navigation, then the river, then, at the bend, the ancient* Unsted Bridge *(look back at it) (350m).*

(i) *Turn R into Unsted Lane (20m) then cross the field R to the corner beyond the barn (150m). Exit via the path to the track near houses (30m) and go R over a rise and down (250m). At the end of the track turn R then L on the fenced path along the fields. Stay on this path to the uphill track after the house L (650m). Turn L* →**(3)**

(2) Cross the Navigation and follow the track past the house L (400m).

(3) At the 4-way junction take the path directly uphill with Unsted Park ahead, Wey valley behind (950m). Over the top, follow the tarmac drive down to the road (150m).

(4) Go L up the road, over the top and halfway down (300m).

(5) Enter the drive R to the house Wood End and take the path L of the garden. Carry on under trees down to the next road in Nursecombe (600m). ☆

(6) Follow the road R until level with Thornecombe Park L (1000m).

(7) Take the tarmac drive R up to Lower Combe Farm (550m) and continue upwards R of the buildings on the track then up the bridleway under trees (550m).

(8) At the 4-way junction take the footpath down R between fences to the road (300m). Cross into the drive opposite. Walk down to the house and on into the valley past the gates of Catteshall Farm (1200m) and Catteshall Manor to the bottom (400m).

(9) Turn L along Catteshall Lane (80m) ✳ then R along Catteshall Road (120m). Walk through the residential area and on along the main road past Catteshall Mill to the bridge at Farncombe Boat House (300m). The **Leathern Bottle** is 200m further on.

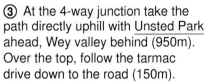

oak apples
actual size

Oak apples are green outgrowths that form in two weeks in May. A 5 mm wasp, *Biorhiza pallida*, lays eggs in a bud, re-programming it to develop into the gall. These eggs are unfertilized but hatch into grubs, about 30 per gall. They emerge in July as 3mm wasps which lay fertilized eggs on the roots and induce 10mm hard root galls to form for over-wintering with one grub each. The females from these grubs lay eggs in buds again. Other species of gall wasp invade the gall, some (inquilines) to share it and others to parasitize the gall-makers.

9 Shalford, Gosden Common and Unsted

About 9 km/5½ miles, undulating, half shady, on the Greensand. The extension of 1¼ km/¾ mile over Chinthurst Hill and the short cut of 3 km/1¾ miles can be used together. OS maps 1:25000 145 Guildford, 1:50000 186 Aldershot.

Start at Shalford, parking in the side road in front of *The Parrot*, SU 998 468. Alternatively start at Chinthurst Hill car park, TQ 014 463.

Linking walks   8❋   10★   11◇   36✿   ⑲◉   ⑳❋   ㉕❋

The Parrot ☎ 01483 561400   ***The Queen Victoria*** ☎ 01483 561733

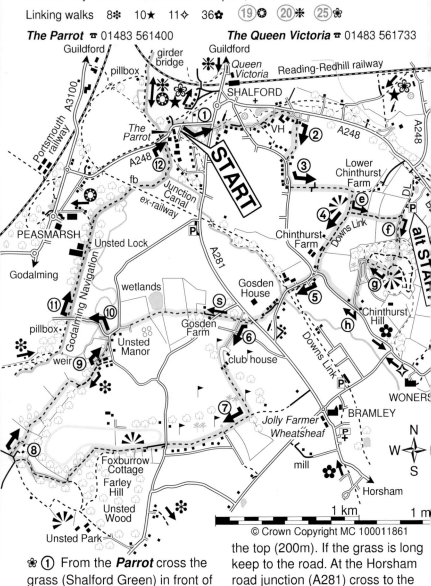

© Crown Copyright MC 100011861

❋ ① From the ***Parrot*** cross the grass (<u>Shalford</u> Green) in front of the pub, curving away from the main road then back towards it at

the top (200m). If the grass is long keep to the road. At the Horsham road junction (A281) cross to the cricket pitch and skirt round the R edge of the main green, over the

lane (200m) and on R of the pond (surrounded by bushes) (200m) into the corner of the green (200m).
② Go past Station Road L, Ashley House R and one more house then turn R on the drive & path between houses to the next road (300m). Go L along it (200m).
③ At the end of the first field L, take the path L between the fields (450m). ✧ After the rise and R curve, turn R on the side path between the fields (150m).
ⓔ *Extension of 1¼ km/¾ miles: At the bridleway (Downs Link) turn L to the T-junction (350m).*
ⓕ *Turn R up* Chinthurst Hill. *Keep to upward paths to the tower on top (450m).* ⩙ *see box Walk 11.*
ⓖ *From the back of the tower opposite the doorway go down the steepest path (200m) and on down the tarmac drive (350m).* ✿
ⓗ *At the road descend R to the next junction (400m). Turn L.* ➔⑤
④ Stay ahead on the DL bridleway down to the road junction (500m).
⑤ Follow Tannery Lane down, initially on top of the L bank. Cross the bridges over the ex- Horsham Railway (now with the Downs Link path) and over Cranleigh Water to Gosden Common (300m). Turn off the road along the R edge of the cricket green (200m). Cross the main road and follow the R path, opposite, to a tarmac drive (100m).
ⓢ *Short cut of 3 km/1¾ miles: Stay ahead over a lane (150m) along Gosden Farm drive (100m), between fields (wetlands R) and along the sewage works drive to the road near Unsted Manor (500m). Go L on the road (100m) and round the R bend.* ❄ ➔⑩

⑥ Go L up the golf club drive, straight up through the sloping car park (350m) and briefly up the drive between huts (50m). Branch off R on the right of way skirting the brow of the hill (350m).
⑦ At the far side, turn R on the boundary path. Stay ahead past the golf course (600m), over the road, up the Foxburrow drive, on beside the wood, past a side path L

> Far R Guildford is visible in the notch where the River Wey cuts through the North Downs ridge between the Hogs Back and Pewley Down. Round R are St Martha's and Chinthurst Hills.

(350m), ❄ round a L bend (150m) into the wood and down steeply to the bridleway junction in the cleft (300m). Turn R down beside the field to the vehicle track (400m) and R down past the house (50m).
⑧ Just after the drive (20m) take the side path R (100m). Go round R & L bends and on between fields at the edge of the Wey floodplain (600m), round R (100m) then L up the farm track (200m).
⑨ At the next house take the side path L to the field (30m) and follow the L edge to the lane (100m). Go L to the road (40m) and L again.
⑩ Step on to the verge to look at Unsted Bridge. Cross it then the River Wey and the Godalming Navigation Bridges (300m).
⑪ Descend to the towpath R and follow it past Unsted Lock (500m), the Peasmarsh path L ✪ (100m), the old Horsham Railway bridge (350m) and the Junction Canal (250m) to the next road (250m). ❄
⑫ Cross to the pavement and go along the road, over the bridge, round to the *Parrot* (100m).

10 Shalford, Chantries and St Martha's Hill

About 7½ km/4¾ miles with a short cut of ¾ km/½ mile; steep slopes, soft sand in summer; long views; bluebells in season; good for winter walking.
OS maps 1:25000 145 Guildford, 1:50000 186 Aldershot.

Start from Chantries car park, Shalford, TQ 003 483 or from St Martha's Hill (Halfpenny Lane) car park, TQ 021 484. Two stations are near the route.

Linking walks   9★   (12)✪   (19)☆   (20)✿   (21)✧   (25)★   (26)✿   (27)✿

The Sea Horse ☎ 01483 514351   *The Queen Victoria* ☎ 01483 561733

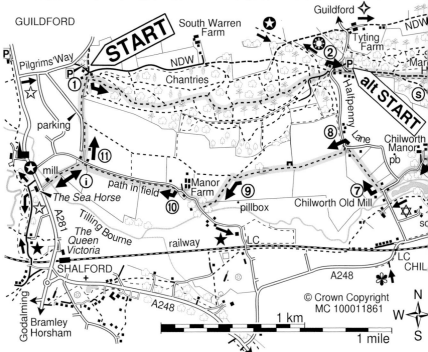

① Just inside Chantries gateway, take the main uphill path away from the fence (not the small path near the garden) onto the ridge. Keep on along the undulating and winding ridgetop always taking the highest onward path until you reach Halfpenny Lane (2000m). ✪
② Walk up the lane L (50m) then R up the footpath (NDW) past houses R and car park L (50m).✧ Go on up St Martha's Hill on the wide sandy track and into the churchyard (W gate) (700m). ✿

Wonersh Shamley Green

Ⓢ *Short cut of ¾ km/½ mile: At the church drop to the S gate and go down the very steep path to the track after the house (550m).* ✦⑥
③ Leave the churchyard by the E gate and stay ahead on the main path over the ironstone outcrop and down the edge of the hill almost to the pillbox L (400m).
④ Turn back R down the broad track (Downs Link), soon between fields (300m). Go round the R bend and on to the L bend (150m).

20

(5) Just round the L bend, look for a path R up into the field above. Follow the L edge of the field to the downhill path (300m). Turn L to the bottom (150m) ✿ then R (50m).

(6) At the wall of Chilworth Manor turn L down the drive to Halfpenny Lane (350m). Stay ahead to the L bend at Blacksmith Lane (150m).

(7) Go up the path above Chilworth Old Mill and out to the lane (400m).

(8) Turn into the field L. Follow the track at the L edge (400m), past farm buildings R, over a rise and into a dip (400m).

(9) Soon after the hillside path back R (40m), take the diverging path L over the field, through the hedge and down steps to the road near the Tilling (300m). ★ Walk up the road R (150m).

(10) Just after the roadside house L is a field gate (30m). Just after that (30m) enter the field L and follow the footpath from field to field beside the hedge beside the lane to the end near houses (600m). ➜(11)

(i) *If visiting the* **Sea Horse** *go down the field L and along the path past* Shalford Mill *(250m) to the road opposite the pub (50m).* ☆❂ *Return the same way to the top.*

(11) Exit from the field, cross the lane and follow the drive opposite. Stay ahead on the footpath then the road outside fields (300m). At the road bend L, diverge R on the path over the foot of the hill to the Chantries car park at the North Downs Way (350m).

R obo̅ ten' de Ricardo Scitsefor. Duo fr̄s tenuer̄ T.R.E.
Vn̄quisq; habuit domū sua. 7 tam manser̄ in una curia.
7 quo uoluer̄ ire potuer̄. Tc 7 m̄ se defd' p.iiii. hid. Tra.e
vi. car'. In d̄nio sunt. ii. car'. 7 xx ix. uilli 7 xi. bord' cū ix.
car'. Ibi æccla 7 x. serui. 7 iii. molini de xvi. sol. 7 iiii. ac̄
p̄a. Silua de xx. porc'.   Debu' h̄s ten un' miles
una v̄. ubi h̄t dim car'. 7 i. seruū 7 v. bord'
Tot T.R.E. ualb. xvi. lib. 7 post: ix. lib. Modo: xx. lib.
huic m̄ pan'una haga in Geldeford. de .iii. sol'.

actual size

The entry for Shalford in the Surrey pages of the Domesday Book, 1086. TRE means before the Conquest, *Tempore Regis Edwardi,* in the time of King Edward. The line through SCALDEFOR was red for highlighting.

Robert holds SCALDEFOR from Richard. Two brothers held it TRE. Each had his own house but they remained in one court. They could go where they would. Then & now it rated for iiii hides. Land for vi ploughs. In demesne are ii ploughs; xxix villeins & xi bordars with ix ploughs. There is a church; x serfs. iii mills @ xvi shillings; iv acres of pasture. Wood @ xx pigs.   Of these hides one man-at-arms holds one virgate, where he has half a plough & i serf & v bordars. Total value TRE xvi pounds; later ix pounds. Now xx pounds. To this manor belongs one property in Guildford @ iii shillings.

11 Chinthurst Hill and Blackheath

About 8 km/5 miles over Greensand hills with good views; short steep slopes; soft sand when dry; half shady. Allow time for confusion on the Blackheath paths. OS maps 1:25000 145 Guildford, 1:50000 186 Aldershot.

Start at Chinthurst Hill car park, TQ 014 462, or Blackheath village, TQ 036 462.

Linking walks 9✧ 10❀ 12★ 36✦ ㉕✧ ㉗✪ ㉜❋

Grantley Arms ☎ 01483 893351

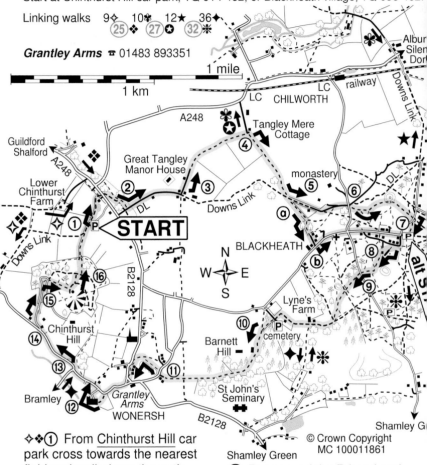

© Crown Copyright MC 100011861

✧❀① From Chinthurst Hill car park cross towards the nearest field and walk down the path beside it to the main road (200m).

② Cross to the path opposite. Follow it obliquely R (200m) and turn L along the lane past the drive of Great Tangley Manor House L (400m) to the 4-way junction of tracks and a path (100m).

③ Turn L past the buildings and go on around the foot of the slope to the cottage at the end (700m). ✪❀

④ Pass round the R bend and ascend between the fields to the level track in the wood (500m).

ⓐ *Equal alternative through* Blackheath *village: Walk straight on between fences (200m). After the R field fork R through the trees and descend past houses (200m).*

ⓑ *Walk up the road L past the church (100m) and crossroads (100m) to the car park (200m).* ✦⑧

22

⑤ Turn L and stay on the track to the road (450m).

⑥ Don't follow the track opposite but take the winding heath path R of it up R of the war memorial on its hillock (250m) ★ and ahead down to the lane (250m).

⑦ On the other side, slightly R (20m), take the path through the trees to the car park (100m). ✳

⑧ Outside the vehicle exit, take the track between the car park and houses to the cricket field (100m) and cross to the pavilion (150m). Turn along that edge of the field away from the houses and go on along the heath path (150m).

⑨ Take the side path R, level with a slight mound L, down to the road (100m). Cross to the path opposite and keep on, over tracks on the ridge (200m) and down the other side to the junction of bridleways outside the corner of the fields (200m). Follow the horse track down between the wood and field, past houses R and the valley path L (200m), ✦ ahead up the sunken track (200m) and round the L bend past the cemetery (50m). Cross the drive from the road and go up the path through the pines (100m).

⑩ Join the track rising from the road and carry on up past Barnett Hill house, over the top and down to the road in Wonersh (850m).

⑪ Cross slightly R to the green and follow the L edge round to the road junction at the Pepper Pot and *Grantley Arms* (350m). Turn R along The Street (200m).

⑫ On the R curve, L of the road, go through the covered gateway (see high frieze) and the memorial garden to the church. Return to the road via the church drive (200m). Carry on (L) along the pavement and out of the village (200m).

⑬ At the bend take the side road R up the hillside. Cranleigh Water is visible below L (350m).

⑭ Between houses on top, bear R up Chinthurst Hill drive (300m).

⑮ Cut across the hairpin bend and take the steepest path up to the tower on top (200m).

With your back to the tower door the great distant eminence almost ahead (SE) is the Leith Hill range. Below, the houses slightly L, are part of Wonersh and above them is Barnett Hill with the eponymous Red Cross house in the trees. Beyond it L, the Blackheath pines are visible further round the ridge. The South Downs are far R.

When you descend: St Martha's Hill is ahead with the North Downs behind it and vehicles climbing to Newlands Corner R. Guildford Cathedral can be seen beyond the Hog's Back through the notch in the chalk ridge with the River Wey. Behind the cathedral is the Tertiary Sands eminence of Bagshot Heath and Swinley Forest in front of Bracknell. The telecommunications mast is 10 miles away at Old Dean.

⑯ The doorway faces SE. Walk northwards over the hill and find paths down towards the L edge of distant St Martha's Hill (300m). From the boundary, walk straight down to the car park (200m).

Great Tangley Manor house is a fine moated Tudor house but only the roof and gables can be seen from outside. The timber framed façade has 1582 incised and curved decorative braces characteristic of eastern England. The Tangley estate was cut from Bramley in the 13th century. This part became *Great* in the 17th century when the land was further subdivided.

12 Blackheath and Albury

About 8¾ km/5½ miles on the Lower Greensand; hilly heath, woodland and pasture. The Blackheath paths are confusing. Shady in summer; good in winter. OS maps 1:25000 145 Guildford, 1:50000 186 Guildford +187 Dorking.

Start from Blackheath village car park, TQ 036 462. Chilworth railway station is fairly near to the route.

Linking walks   11★   ㉖❀   ㉗✚   ㉘✳   ㉚✡   ㉜✳

The Drummond Arms ☎ 01483 202039   **The Percy Arms** ☎ 01483 561765

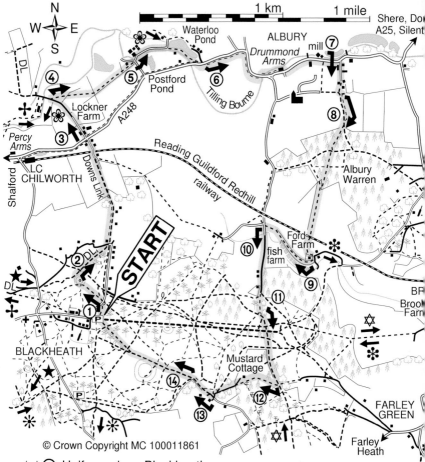

© Crown Copyright MC 100011861

★★① Halfway along Blackheath village car park take the slightly rising path (120m). Turn R on the road (20m) and L on the first path opposite. Avoid the R fork and keep on through heath, soon rising, to the memorial on the hillock (200m).

② Go over the top of the hillock and straight down the other side to the bridleway (50m). Bear R on the bridleway, across a junction (40m) and stay ahead to the corner of the heath near houses (300m). Cross

24

the track to the path beside the garden and keep on down the hillside then on tarmac over the railway to the A248 (800m). (The **Percy Arms** and Chilworth Station are 500m L along the road.)

③ Cross and walk down the drive past Lockner Farm (400m). ❀

④ Just before the bridge turn off back R through the fields (site of the Admiralty gunpowder works), past a pond far L and a garden to Postford Pond (650m).

⑤ Follow the lane over the bridge L, past offices (which replaced Postford Mill) and on (250m). At the bend take the path R between the ponds (or the next path R) to the main road (250m).

⑥ Follow the pavements L all the way to the **Drummond Arms** in Albury (700m). Carry on through the village past the mill L (300m) and the trout pond L (150m).

⑦ Where the road bends L, turn R into the estate yard (if the office is open ask to see the pigeon house) then follow the drive to the top and go on up the path (200m).

⑧ At the path junction in the wood either go on up the sunken track or, better, climb to the corner of the field above L and follow the edge above the sunken track, rejoining it at the gate near the top (200m). Just before the wood, fork R out of the sunken track over the hilltop (200m). Cross a track and carry on down to the edge of the plantation (300m). In the field go L along the fence past the corner of the wood and straight down to the railway (300m). Cross the lines and descend into the sunken path which curves L past the garden of Ford Farm house (150m). ✳

⑨ At the drive turn R (10m) and R again into the field. Stay beside the lynchet on the valleyside to the next lane (450m).

⑩ Turn L over the brook. Keep on up the sandy lane to the last house (500m) ✿ and straight up the middle path (200m).

⑪ Over the brow, bear L on the cross track which curves R and crosses several level forest tracks (200m). Stay ahead to the next brow (150m) and down to the crossing public footpath (100m).

⑫ Turn back R up the slope past Mustard Cottage R (250m) and carry on ahead on the sandy drive (other tracks join R) round down L to the drive junction (250m).

⑬ Turn R. Follow the boundary track until it bends L (200m). ✳

⑭ Take the straight track ahead through the heath, over a rise (300m) and on (200m). At the crossing track just before the next rise, fork R to the car park (200m).

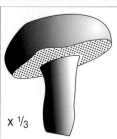

Boletus has many species which grow on heaths and are easily recognised: mainly brown with stout stalks, deep caps and pores in place of gills. Most are edible (they are canned in Poland); one is poisonous. Their hyphae (threads) attach them to birch or conifer roots, for mutual benefit, in the symbiotic partnership called *mycorrhiza*. Fungi are like plants and animals in their DNA but best considered a kingdom themselves, with the moulds and yeasts. Bacteria have different DNA.

x ⅓

13 Elstead, Puttenham Common and Rodsall

About 9¼ km/5¾ miles with a short cut of 1¼ km/¾ mile; mainly farmland but with confusing heath and woodland; fairly shady; soft sand in summer; bluebells in season. OS maps 1:25000 145 Guildford, 1:50000 186 Aldershot.

Start at Elstead, parking in the long layby near the church, SU 905 435, or from a Puttenham Common car park, Middle, SU 912 458 or Top, SU 920 461.

Linking walks 1✦ 6❀ 14✪
21★ 22✪ 23✿ 27♣

The Woolpack 01252 703106
Elstead Mill 01252 703333
The Golden Fleece
01252 702349

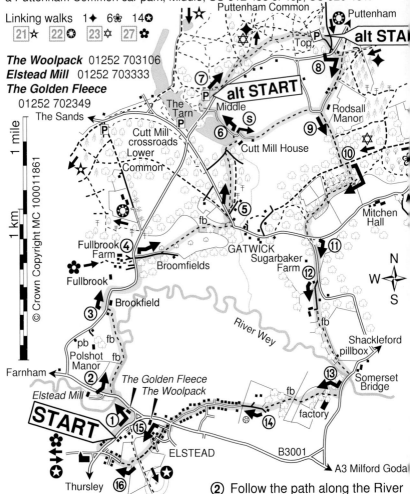

① From the Elstead layby walk along the road to the village green (300m)(the **Woolpack** is 100m R). Bear L past the shops and L along the main road. Cross the bridge to the river bank path R (350m). Before following it cross the road into the drive to see Elstead Mill.

② Follow the path along the River Wey and ahead to the road (650m).
③ Turn R up the road which winds R then L past Fulbrook (500m). ✪✿
④ Opposite Fullbrook Farm turn R on the Broomfields track to the gate L (200m). Cross the field ½L from the track (300m) and go on through trees to the road at Gatwick (250m).

26

⑤ Turn L to the track R after the house (50m). Take the footpath diverging R of the road and fork L over Lower Puttenham Common (400m). Cross the track at the bend and go along the dam of Cutt Mill Pond, round the corner to the boat house and onto the drive (120m).

Ⓢ *Short cut of 1¼ km/¾ mile: Turn R along the winding drive to the cottage (150m). Stay ahead on the path to the next lane (400m) and turn R to the bend (100m).* ➔⑨

⑥ Turn L along the drive to the road (250m). Cross into the trees opposite and ascend R beside the old sandpit to the car park. Cross to the road exit (200m). ✿◆✫

⑦ At Puttenham Common Middle Car Park take the path up beside the road soon diverging from it (300m). Just after the cross paths fork R and stay ahead until you see a wide steep path ½R (400m). Top car park is on top (100m).

⑧ From Puttenham Common Top car park go out to the road (100m). Cross to the house and skirt R of the garden into the sunken track (100m). Go R to the tarmac and ahead past Rodsall Manor House (300m) to the first bend (100m).

⑨ At the bend go down the side path. Stay ahead into the wood to the T-junction (400m). ❀

⑩ Slightly L (30m) take the path on the other side to the crosspath just before the field (150m). Turn R. Keep near the L edge of the wood past conifers L and paddocks far R (400m). Near the end of the field turn into it and go R round the edge to the road junction (100m).

⑪ Follow Attleford Lane opposite past Sugar Baker Farm R (400m).

⑫ At the first roadside house bear R along the farm track. After the buildings keep on slightly L into the wood, over the footbridge, past a pillbox and across the field to Somerset Bridge (550m).

⑬ Go over the bridge, up the road (150m), R on the first side track and on through the trees (150m). At the field turn L and converge on the R edge (150m). At the corner take the path under trees (300m).

⑭ Join the track and continue between the houses on Ham Lane into Elstead (650m).

⑮ Cross the main road into the road opposite (30m). Turn R along Back Lane past one house (40m) then L up the hill to the staggered cross path on top (400m). ✪

⑯ Avoid the path L. Go down outside (L of) the field and on to the crossroads at Elstead Church (200m) ✿ then R to the layby.

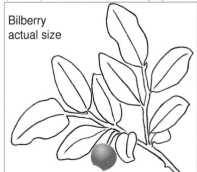

Bilberry
actual size

Bilberry, *Vaccinium myrtillus*, is an undershrub up to 50cm/2ft. In Surrey heaths it is usually on slopes under pines. Leafless in winter, the plants become a tangle of angular bright green twigs. The blue-black berries, eaten in late summer and the small globular white flowers in May hang under the foliage. *Hurts*, a Surrey dialect word for the fruit, explains names like Hurtwood and Hurtmore.

14 The Moat, the Lion's Mouth and Elstead

About 8¾ km/5½ miles with an extension of ¾ km/½ mile; confusing heath with little shade; several short steep ascents; soft sand in summer, wading in very wet seasons. OS maps 1:25000 145 Guildford 1:50000 186 Aldershot.

Start from The Moat car park, SU 899 416, or in Elstead, SU 905 435, at the long layby between the village green and the church on the Thursley road.

The Woolpack ☎ 01252 703106   Linking 13❂ 15✳ 16❖ 27✿ 28✦ 30✲
The Golden Fleece ☎ 01252 702349
Elstead Mill ☎ 01252 703333

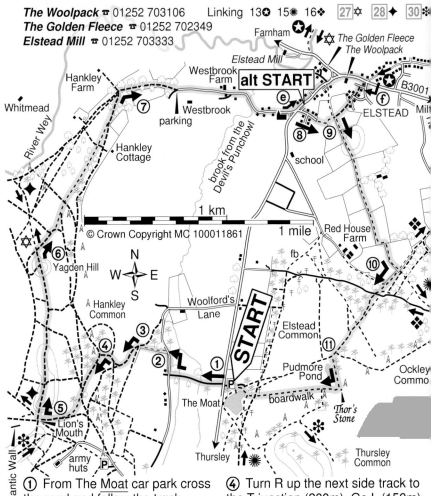

① From The Moat car park cross the road and follow the track, opposite, to the end (400m).

② Follow the lane R. Watch out for the end of the fence L (150m). Go L along it under the trees (200m).

③ Emerging on the open heath of Hankley Common, turn L along the major vehicle track (250m).

④ Turn R up the next side track to the T-junction (200m). Go L (150m) and diverge R on the track curving up though the trees ✦ (If confused or for a short cut, go straight up through the heather to the ridge top.) Keep on up to the sandy cleft in the ridge. This is the Lion's Mouth (400m).

⑤ Climb onto the gravel ridge R and go north along it (towards the distant telecommunications tower at Crooksbury Hill), then down a bit and up over Yagden Hill (1100m).✿

⑥ From the brow descend the N path (80m) then turn R down the track at the foot. When it curves R (200m) stay ahead, under the power cables (200m). Disregard tracks L & R and continue to the 5-way junction under trees (800m).

⑦ Disregard the track to Hankley Farm ahead. Turn R on the main track and continue on the lane past Westbrook Farm to Elstead Church and the road junction (1400m).

ⓔ *Extension of ¾ km/½ mile to the village green and pubs: Turn L to the Green ❖ and the **Woolpack** (400m). Carry on along the main road, B3001 (200m).*

ⓕ *Turn R at the next side road, Springfield, and R again into Back Lane then take the path L, after the first house, up the hill to the 4-way junction on top (400m). Turn L.* ➔⑨

⑧ Cross the road and walk up West Hill (150m) then up the path beside the field to the track junction on top (100m). Turn R .

⑨ Follow the footpath along the R edge of the fields to the wood on the Common (1200m). ✳❖

⑩ Just before the gate into the wood, take the track R under trees to the broad gravelled track (250m). Cross and continue ahead on the horse track over the heath to Pudmore Pond L (500m). You should be walking almost parallel with cables on pylons 400m L.

⑪ Just before Pudmore Pond are two side paths L, 30m apart. Take the 2nd, with pines, along the boundary mound of Thursley Common and round the bend at Thor's Stone (200m). ✳ Go on straight over Thursley Bog along the boardwalk on the boundary mound (600m). Cross the path with electricity poles to a T-junction (100m) then go R round the Moat pond to the car park (150m).

Thursley Common has the richest dragonfly and damsel-fly fauna in Britain. These two groups make up the insect order Odonata. They are the hawks of the insect world and catch other insects on the wing with forward mounted legs. The juveniles are wingless and aquatic, preying on water insects and crustaceans.

Slender form distinguishes damsel-flies, but they may be longer than small dragonflies. The classification is based on wing form. Dragonflies have different front and hind wings which are spread at rest. Damsel-flies have similar wings fore and aft, pressed together when perched.

Dragonflies of Great Britain & Ireland
Cyril O Hammond Harley rev 1996 116pp

15 Thursley Common and Village

About 8½ km/5¼ miles; confusing heath, woodland and ponds; best when the heather is in flower; soft sand in summer; good for birds, dragonflies and repiles. OS maps 1:25000 145 Guildford +133 Haslemere, 1:50000 186 Aldershot.

Start from The Moat (pond) car park, SU 899 416, or at Thursley recreation ground, SU 899 398, or at the Old Portsmouth Road parking area, SU 497 394.

Linking walks 14✻ 16✦ 18✿ 19✻ 30★ 32✾

The Three Horseshoes
☎ 01252 703268

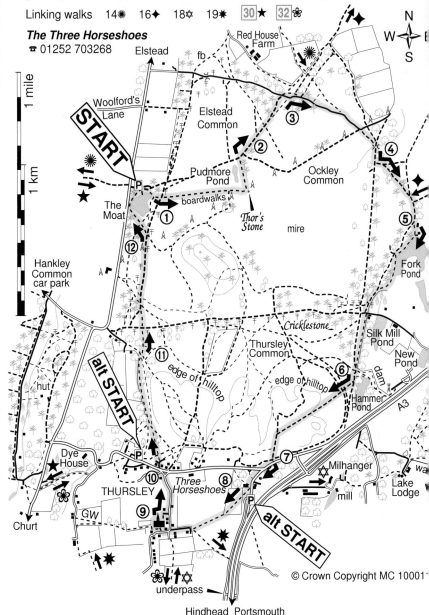

© Crown Copyright MC 10001

Hindhead Portsmouth

✱① At The Moat follow the pond edge away from the road round the corner (150m) then take the path L to the sandy track near electicity posts (50m). On the other side take the Nature Reserve footpath (with signs), on boardwalks, along an ancient boundary mound. Disregard side boardwalks (600m). After Pudmore Pond L keep on round the L bend at Thor's Stone to the parallel horse track (200m).

② Follow the heath track R to the hard, gravelled track (500m). ✦

③ Go R along the track, around L & R bends and on to the L bend just after the pylons (600m). Don't follow this bend but continue ahead over the stream (200m).

④ After the stream (100m), take the branch track L (50m) then turn off R. Pass a path converging L and the nearby fenced track L ✪ (250m) and keep on (150m).

⑤ Where the path bends slightly R, fork L on the lesser path to Fork Pond (100m). Stay at the edge of the pond to the end when the boundary forces you back to the main path (400m). When this path bends R (200m) keep to the lesser path along the boundary past the house and re-join the main track where the boundary bends L (400m). Stay ahead past side paths L until the Hammer Pond is visible L (100m). ✿

⑥ Fork R up the side path which crosses two curving paths (100m) and ascends the hill. This was the London to Portsmouth Road! On the brow (250m) look back then continue over the flat top to the edge of Thursley Common (450m).

⑦ Cross the boundary track and go out to the road (20m). Turn R (50m) then fork L down the Old Portsmouth Road (200m).

⑧ Opposite the houses L (former *Red Lion*), near the shed, take the oblique path across the fields to a corner (250m) and carry on up the next field to the house (250m). ✱ Walk down the drive to the bend in the lane (150m) and ahead up to Thursley Church (100m). ★✿

⑨ Walk round the church and leave by the back gate (N) (100m). Turn L along the lane to Street House. Fork L at the end (300m). The *Three Horseshoes* is 150m R.

⑩ Cross the road into the track between houses. When it bends R (30m) go down the side path ahead, with paths converging R&L, to the field (300m). Carry on beside it or on the parallel path R (500m).

⑪ When the path bends L at the end of the field branch off on the path ahead over the wide sandy track (200m). Carry on (500m).

⑫ After the pylons bear L on the oblique cross path and follow it L of The Moat to the car park (300m).

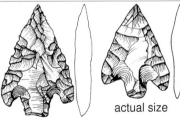

actual size

Flint arrow heads found on the slopes of Thursley Common by local people. They are Neolithic style but working in flint persisted well into the Bronze Age. Dating to 2000BC approximate.

Drawn by Audrey Graham

© Surrey Archæological Collections v86 1999

16 Rodborough, Ockley and Royal Commons

About 7½ km/4½ miles with an extension of 1 km/¾ mile; confusing heath and woodland, half shady. OS maps 1:25000 145 Guildford 1:50000 186 Aldershot.

Start at Rodborough Common car park, SU 937 418, reached from the access road to the A3 south from Milford.

Linking walks   14❖ 15✦ 17✳

The White Lion ☎ 01483 421116

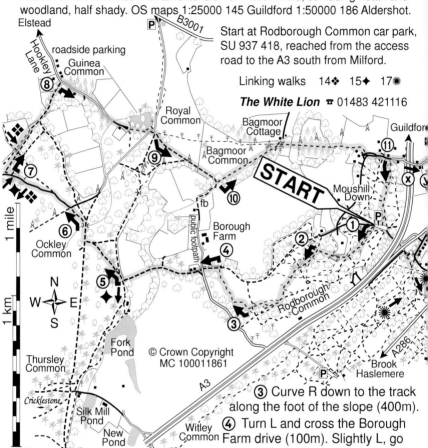

③ Curve R down to the track along the foot of the slope (400m).

④ Turn L and cross the Borough Farm drive (100m). Slightly L, go on past the houses and eventually between fields to the boundary track of Ockley Common (600m).✦

⑤ Turn R (70m) and fork L up to the T-junction (300m). Turn L to the broad sandy path (50m) and follow it R to the stream (100m).

⑥ After the culvert, fork L to the hard track (150m) and follow that ahead to the S-curve (500m). ❖

⑦ Just into the trees on the bend (3m) turn R on the track parallel with a boundary mound (200m). At the field gateway transfer to the parallel path, 10m L at the edge of

① At Rodborough Common car park walk to the inner end and take the side path L, either fork, level at first (200m) then down to the 4-way junction in trees opposite a house 100m R (100m). Bear R down past the garden fence and earthworks to the cross path near the bottom of the dip (200m).

② Turn L. Pass lots of side paths and join the converging path on a rise into trees (400m). Carry on to the top (100m) then diverge R on the parallel path outside the trees and cross the valley path (100m).

© Crown Copyright MC 100011861

the field, rejoining the track after the field (150m). Carry on down past a side track R (80m), to Hookley Lane with houses (300m).

⑧ Turn R on the road through Guinea Common (450m). Continue on the drive through the garden at the end (100m) then on the path in the trees to the end of the pond in Royal Common (200m).

⑨ Cross the drive to the track junction (30m R of power cables) (30m). Take the public footpath (ie between the path parallel with the electricity posts and the track diverging from the drive)(550m).

⑩ At the T-junction turn L through Bagmoor Common, eventually crossing the footbridge 50m R of Bagmore Cottage (500m). Stay ahead over the fields (100m) then between tree plantations (250m) and along the track between fields to house drives (200m). Go up the L slope (30m) and L on the unmade road to the first house R (200m).

ⓧ *Extension of 1 km/¾ miles to Moushill Manor and the White Lion: Continue on the winding road over the A3 to the high garden wall L in trees (350m) and turn off R on Moushill Manor drive. Go past the house and on along the drive of the next house to the road (300m).*

ⓘ *If going to the* **White Lion** *turn L along the pavement (150m). Return the same way. If not,*

ⓨ *Turn R along the pavement to the R curve (200m) then diverge L along the unmade road past houses to the bend (250m).*

ⓩ *Take the path ahead into the trees (50m). Turn R on the first side path, past the building (pump station) to the road (100m). Cross to the path opposite and follow it to the tunnel under the A3 (30m). Go through to the car park (150m).*

⑪ 30m before this house turn R up the path to the top of Moushill Down (150m). Stay ahead down to the car park (300m). ✳

Commons are usually open to the public for air and exercise but are not owned by the public or by the nation. They are remnants of land called *waste* in early documents which was not ploughed for crops but used for grazing, firewood, peat cutting, building materials, etc. As the population grew, the waste was sub-divided between communities who marked boundaries with mounds in medieval times. The land now belonged to the lord of the manor and commoners; they could use it for themselves but could not work it for private profit or sell it.

To promote enterprise there was a tendency from the Middle Ages onwards for shared arable land to be parcelled and enclosed by agreement into farms and much of the waste was taken up in the process. If commoners resisted, they were overcome, later on, by Enclosure Acts. Usually, only village greens and the least useful commons survived. Surrey has large commons because of its poor soils and extensive heaths on the Tertiary Sands and Lower Greensand.

In the 20th century commons lost sight of their commoners; a commoner might have rights to graze two cows but was not allowed to fence them and would not want to herd them; coal replaced peat and firewood; etc. By default, lords of the manor became the only visible owners and were able to dispose of commons. In Surrey they sold to boroughs, builders, the Army, preservation societies and Forestry Commission. There are still a few commoners with registered rights.

The Common Lands of England & Wales W G Hoskins & L Dudley Stamp 1963 Collins

17 Witley Common and Mare Hill.

About 7½ km/4¾ miles with an extension of 2 km/1¼ miles. Confusing heath; best when the heather is in flower (August); half shady, gentle slopes. OS maps 1:25000 145 Guildford, 1:50000 186 Aldershot.

Start at Webb Road car park, SU 933 409. There are other car parks on the route: Lea Coach Road, SU 927 398, next to the cemetery at Milford Common, SU 941 413, and Roke Lane on Mare Hill, SU 937 399. Rodborough Common car park is near the extension, SU 937 418.

Linking walks 16✿ 18✳ 21✳

The White Lion
☎ 01483 421116

The Star
☎ 01428 684656

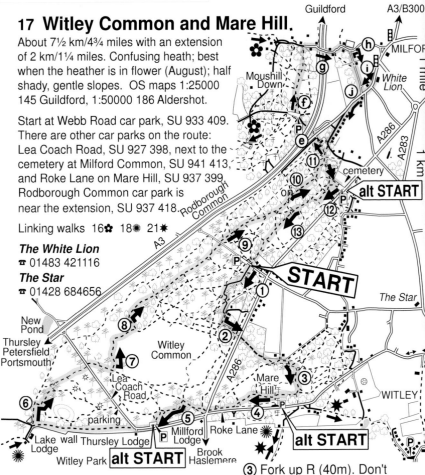

① From Webb Road car park take the main hard path to the National Trust Witley Centre, passing round R & L bends (450m).

② Turn R on the path crossing the end of the building. The path runs beside a boundary mound (70m). When it ends don't continue ahead but turn L. Follow the lesser path R of the mound then diverge R to the road (150m) and continue up the track opposite to the corner of a garden (200m). Stay ahead in the trees outside the gardens past the paths from the road L (120m) to the next path junction (40m).

③ Fork up R (40m). Don't follow the L bend but the path ahead (80m). Turn R up the steep side path to the ridge track (200m) then R to the summit of Mare Hill (150m) (car park 80m L). ✳✳

④ Stay on the ridge path down to the road junction (500m). Cross the A286 into the trees opposite (40m) then fork L to the first cross path (150m). Go L, round R & L bends, to the road at the car park (300m).

⑤ Walk along the road R to the bend at the Thursley gatehouse of Witley Park (120m) then take the path ahead under trees outside the wall to the unmade road (700m).

34

⑥ Take the path R next to the road (150m) and turn up the first side path R to the track round the hillock (50m) (of the Herpetological Conservation Trust). Go L round the slope watching for a side path back L (150m). Cross L to the parallel path (70m) and go R on that past a side path R (100m) and, Bronze Age barrow R to the road (250m). Opposite take the path to the first cross path (200m).

⑦ Turn L. The path bends R (200m) to a T-junction (150m).

⑧ Turn L. Follow the path round a R bend (100m) then stay ahead, almost in a straight line straight to Webb Road (disused part) (800m).

⑨ There are two paths opposite. Take the L one. Watch out for the junction with a converging path R (350m). Stay ahead past another converging path R (80m) to the fork at the start of a L curve (150m).

⑩ Fork R. Stay ahead down past a cross path (250m) and over a rise to a side path back R, 20m from a large sand pit R (100m).

➔⑪ Turn back R or ➔ⓔ ahead:

ⓔ *Extension of 2 km/1¼ miles to Moushill Down and the White Lion: Stay ahead (70m). Watch out for a building L and fork L on the path past it to the road (100m). Cross. Follow the path opposite to the tunnel under the A3 (30m). Go through to Rodborough Common car park (100m).* ✿

ⓕ *Near the middle of the car park take the side path into the trees. Stay ahead to the top of Mousehill Down (450m) and down the other side to the houses (150m).*

ⓖ *Go R over the A3 to the high garden wall L in trees (350m).*

ⓗ *Turn R along the Moushill Manor drive. Go past the house and on along the drive of the next house to the road (300m).*

ⓘ *If going to the **White Lion** turn L along the pavement (150m). Return the same way. If not,*

ⓙ *Turn R along the pavement to the R curve (200m) then diverge L on the unmade road past houses to the bend (250m). Take the path ahead up through the trees (150m) and fork L near the sandpit.*

⑪ Stay on this path, avoiding side paths R (100m), to the Milford Common car park (100m).

⑫ Leave the car park by the path which is not beside the cemetery (60m). Turn L on the first cross path and follow it round a R bend (100m) to a T-junction (50m). Turn L up through the trees (150m).

⑬ Just after the trees fork L. Stay ahead to Webb Road near the parking area (500m).

Mare Hill is a part of Witley Common owned by Waverley Borough. The abrupt heath/field transition near Roke Lane is caused by a geological fault which brings the fertile Bargate stratum against acid sands.

Witley is rated in the Domesday Book @ 20 hides, a large manor. A *hide* is bluntly interpreted as 120 acres of land which is misleading. Only arable land was quantified in hides and an estate usually had permanent pasture and *waste* like the Common. Estate comparisons ancient and modern suggest hides varied which may be why an 11th century will needed to define a hide as 120 acres. In the Domesday Book, hidage is notional - a rateable value. The Hundred, part of a county from 11th to 19th century, probably originated as 100 hides.

18 Brook, Witley Park and Thursley

About 8 km/5 miles, with an extension of 4¼ km/2¾ miles to Thursley; heath, pasture and woodland; short steep ascents. The heaths are confusing.
OS maps 1:25000 145 Guildford +133 Haslemere, 1:50000 186 Aldershot.

Start from Brook, parking in the side road opposite the pub, SU 930 380.
On the extension, Thursley car park is close to the route, SU 900 398.

Linking walks 15✿ 17✱ 19✽ 20★ 21★ 23☆ 30❖ 32✾

Dog & Pheasant 01428 682763
Three Horseshoes 01252 703268

① At Brook enter the cricket field opposite the **Dog & Pheasant**. Go round the wall L and on into the wood to the tarmac drive (350m).

② Follow the Greensand Way: Cross the main road and walk along the side road beside the wall (400m). At Pine Lodge, the first house R, go through the wall, up the hill and between fields (250m).

③ Turn R down the track. Stay ahead into the valley (300m), up to the wall (150m), over the drive of the next house, through small fields (200m), over the drive of Heath Hall and up into the field.

④ Turn R along the edge and go round a corner (200m) then cross the fence and follow it L (150m).

ⓔ *Extension of 4¼ km/2¾ miles: Cross the road. Go straight over the field (120m), obliquely down the slope (100m), ✽ R on the path at the foot, across the valley and up Cosford Farm drive (200m).*

ⓕ *At the R bend bear L down the track to a 4-way junction (500m). ★ Stay ahead along the farm drive (120m). Just before the house turn R up the oblique track (80m). At the fields take the oblique uphill branch track to a junction (100m) and continue up into the top field (20m). Keep on obliquely to the hilltop then beside the A3 (150m).*

ⓖ *Pass under the A3 (70m). Turn R down the little road (40m) and L into the field. ✾✽ Cross obliquely to the gate under trees at the bottom corner (350m). Go through the next field parallel with the L edge (250m) and on down the fields to Thursley (500m). ❖ Stay ahead (R) on the lane to the end past Street House (400m). ✿ (**Three Horseshoes** R)*

ⓗ *Over the road from the R outlet, take the path between the houses (200m). After the field go R along the edge of Thursley Common (400m), round curves R&L (150m) and on near the road downhill to the exit at the road bridge (400m).*

① Cross the A3 (150m) and go R down the slip road (150m). Halfway down turn L on the tarmac drive then L down the farm track (250m). Stay ahead down the Millhanger drive, round the valley past Cosford Mill R (200m), up the path (150m) and ahead on the road (100m). →⑥

round a L bend to the next cross path (200m). Turn R (100m) and fork L to the A286 (80m). Continue over the A286 up the path parallel with Roke Lane. Stay on the main path up Mare Hill past the summit cross path (500m) to the next path junction (150m).

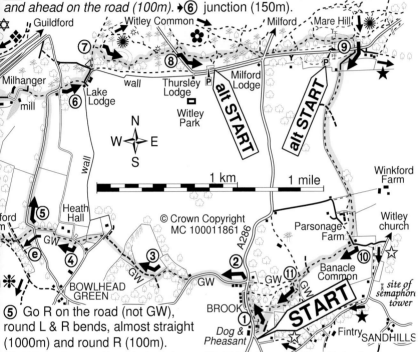

© Crown Copyright MC 100011861

⑤ Go R on the road (not GW), round L & R bends, almost straight (1000m) and round R (100m).

⑥ When the road bends L at the farm drive, take the path ahead down to the house (200m). Go down the drive (100m). At the two footpaths R on the bend, take the one away from the Witley Park wall to the first side path R (150m). ✻

⑦ Turn R up towards the hillock (HerpetologicalCT). Follow the path over the R flank and down past the side path at the Bronze Age barrow (500m) to Lea Coach Road (150m).

⑧ Cross into the next part of Witley Common (50m). Take the path R up round the top (300m), over a cross path (car park R) and

⑨ Take the path R to Roke Lane (80m). ★ Opposite, go down the drive (200m). Stay ahead past the house to the fields and up the dry valley (1000m). In the narrow field L of the farm make for the R corner near the next house (150m). Turn L between the cottages (50m). ☆

⑩ At the bend turn R on the path between fields to the wood (450m).

⑪ Into the trees (50m) take the 1st side path (GW) back to the L field (60m) then turn R across the wood. Follow the path down and along the hill then down L to the cricket field (250m). Cross to the road (150m).

37

19 Thursley, Emley Farm and Highfield Farm

About 9 km/5¾ miles. The extension of 2¼ km/1¼ miles and short cut of 4 km/2½ miles can be used together; hilly farm land on the Greensand with lots of stiles. OS maps 1:25000 133 Haslemere, 1:50000 186 Aldershot.

Start at Thursley recreation ground, SU 900 398, near the children's play area.

Linking walks 15✳ 18✳ 20❉ 30◇ 32✳ 33✿

The Three Horseshoes ☎ 01252 703268

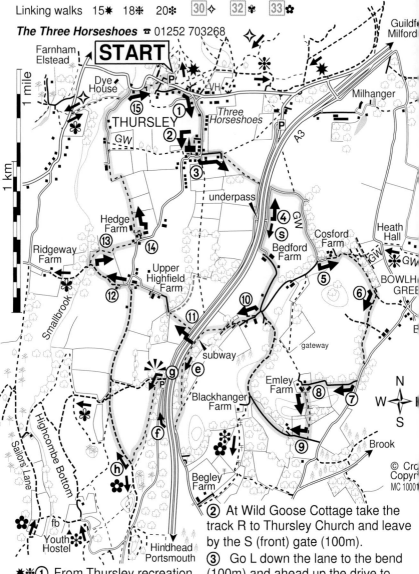

② At Wild Goose Cottage take the track R to Thursley Church and leave by the S (front) gate (100m).

③ Go L down the lane to the bend (100m) and ahead up the drive to the field (150m). ✳ Two paths cross obliquely. Take the R one across the R corner then along the edge R

✳✳**①** From Thursley recreation ground walk into the village (100m) and turn R past Street House down The Street (300m).

(400m). Turn R up the narrow road beside the A3 (200m) then pass under the A3 (50m).

(S) *Short cut of 4 km/2½ miles: Turn R up the drive (250m). On top go round L & R bends and down the cart track past the farm to the 4-way junction (400m) then R.* ✦⑩

④ Go L down the drive (200m), round the R bend and on over the rise through the trees (650m).

⑤ Carry on round the L bend to Cosford Farm (60m). At the bend in the drive, stay ahead down the track, over the stream (100m) then fork R gently up between the hillside wood L and fields R (350m).

⑥ Soon after the end of the wood turn R up the cross track between fields (200m). Continue over the cross track up to the road (200m). Go up the road R (100m).

⑦ Turn R on the next drive. Keep on to Emley Farm (400m).

⑧ Opposite the house R take the footpath L beside the 2nd barn, up over the hilltop and down through the trees (200m). Go down the next field to the next farm drive (100m).

⑨ Turn R past houses R (150m). When the drive bends down L to Blackhanger Farm (350m),✾✿ stay ahead on the track into the trees, round down past the pond L, over the causeway dam (550m) and up to a 4-way junction (150m). Turn L.

⑩ Follow the track into the farm (120m). Just before the house bear R up the oblique track (100m). At the fields take the oblique uphill branch track to a junction (100m) and continue up the path into the top field (20m). Keep on obliquely (L) to the hilltop then beside the A3 to the subway (200m).

ⓔ *Extension of 2¼ km/1¼ miles: Stay ahead L of the A3 and down to the minor road (650m)*

ⓕ *Go under the A3 and up the road to the lane junction L (300m).*

ⓖ *Soon after the junction (50m) turn L up the track, beside a field (60m) and take the first side track up through Hindhead Common to the major track on the edge of the Devil's Punch Bowl (600m).* ✿

ⓗ *Turn R on this track down through the heath (450m)* ✾ *Stay ahead past fields to the lane junction (800m) then turn L.* ✦⑫

⑪ Pass under the A3 (70m). Turn R between the roads (40m) and L into the field. Go straight across aiming for the gap in the trees in the dip (300m). Join the track and follow it up R of the barn. At the next R bend diverge L on the footpath through the stable yard to the lane junction (400m). Cross.

⑫ Follow the lane away from the farm. When it bends L stay ahead, R of the house, down the steep track to Smallbrook (300m). ✾

⑬ Don't cross but ascend R to the fields above the stream and follow the winding path outside the fields to the road (450m).

⑭ Turn L on the road but almost immediately (30m) take the footpath L from the drive of Hedge Farm. Go round the garden (100m) then R, down between the fields, with L & R bends, to the lane (600m). ✧ Keep on ahead down to the road (600m).

⑮ Follow the road R until it bends L uphill (100m) then go straight up the path ahead and over the road to the recreation ground (200m).

20 The Devil's Punch Bowl and Highfield Farm

About 9½ km/6 miles with a short cut of 1½ km/1 mile;
heath, pasture, woodland; long ascents; lots of stiles.
OS maps 1:25000 133 Haslemere, 1:50000 186 Aldershot.

Start at Hindhead from the National Trust car park (pay),
SU 890 357, almost opposite the Devil's Punch Bowl Hotel.

Linking walks 18❋ 19❋
30◇ 32★ 33◆

Devil's Punch Bowl Hotel
☎ 01428 606565
Devil's Punch Bowl Café
☎ 01428 608771

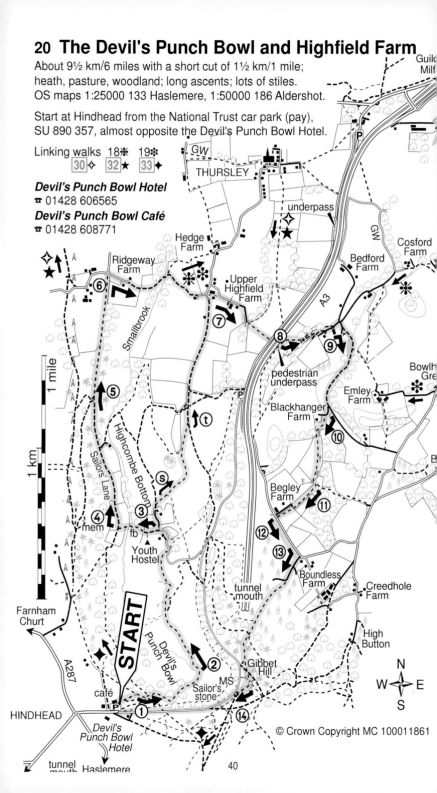

© Crown Copyright MC 100011861

① From the Hindhead NT car park take the gravel path R of the *café* to the view point on the rim of the Devil's Punch Bowl (100m). Turn R on the path below it (120m) then L downhill. Avoid a steeper side path back L (30m) ✦ and carry on to the bend (150m) then down L to the spring in the narrow valley (350m).

② Carry on ahead, undulating around the side of the combe, disregarding all side tracks (800m). At the end go L down the tarmac lane past houses and round a L curve to a R bend (200m).

Ⓢ *Short cut of 1½ km/1 mile: Stay on the drive down past the cottage (200m). After the cattle grid bear R on the path up the combe-side to the track on top (700m).*

Ⓣ *On the ridge track go L down to the lane (900m) then R. ✦⑦*

③ Don't follow the R bend of the drive but stay ahead down the track below the Youth Hostel, over Smallbrook (200m) and up steeply to the T-junction (100m).

④ Turn R and follow the track past fields (500m) and ahead up the flank of the valley (400m). ★✧

⑤ When the main track bends L on top, take the (R) side path ahead along the ridge; the horse track soon sinks into a deep stony cleft between fields, at first grey Hythe sandstone then brown Bargate sandstone (800m).

⑥ At the lane go R up past the houses and on down the rocky track to the stream (450m). ✲✲ On the other side, stay on the track up to a house drive and on to the lane junction (300m). Stay ahead.

⑦ Take the footpath through the Highfield stableyard to the farm track and carry on past another house and down (400m). At the bottom enter the field L and go straight up the slope and over to the main road, the A3 (300m).

⑧ Cross the little road and turn R to the subway (50m). Go under the A3 and turn L on the path which curves R and descends obliquely down the field to the exit near the middle of the bottom edge (150m). Carry on down through the trees to the farm house (150m) and walk out along the drive L (100m).

⑨ At the track junction go R, past the pond (200m) and on to Blackhanger Farm (500m).

⑩ Turn R down the drive (100m). Just before the garden enter the field L and skirt the garden to the top corner (100m). Cross the belt of trees L to the next field (40m) and follow the L edge (300m).

⑪ At the end, exit L to the path junction (30m) then go R along the boundary (200m). Cross the last field to the R corner (100m).

⑫ Join the lane and walk L to Boundless Farm (300m).

⑬ Just before the first house turn R up the track (200m). At the R curve keep on up the lesser track ahead, over a crosspath (400m) and round L. When the path flattens, ignore a side path R and cross a track (250m) then ascend to the flat top of Gibbet Hill (100m).

⑭ From the trig point take the level track (SW) to the tarmac drive on the edge of the hill (Old Portsmouth Road)(120m). Go L down it, past the murdered sailor's stone R (100m), to the end at the car park in Hindhead (700m). The *Devil's Punch Bowl* Hotel is L (50m).

21 Witley, Enton and Sandhills

About 8½ km/5¼ miles with an extension of 700m around Banacle Common; undulating farmland and wood with one short steep ascent; half shady; suitable for winter walking. OS maps 1:25000 133 Haslemere, 1:50000 186 Aldershot.

Start from Witley Lodge, SU 945 39, near Witley Church or the car park near Sweetwater Pond, SU 953 390. Witley Station (in Wormley), SU 948 379, has free parking at weekends.

Linking walks 17✸ 18★ 22✿ 23♣ 24✸ 28✿

The White Hart ☎ 01428 682554
The Star ☎ 01428 684656

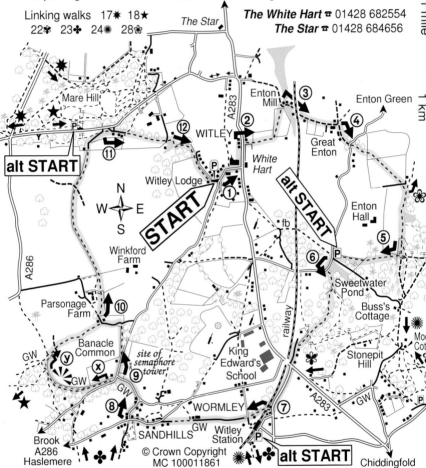

① From Witley Lodge walk down the road past the church to the A283 at the **White Hart** (200m). Follow the pavement L and cross at the end of the high wall (150m).

② Follow the footpath between the wall and house (50m) and ahead and through fields (150m).

Turn L into the long field and diverge from the L edge down to the L house (200m).

③ Outside turn R on the track over Enton millstream R. Keep on winding past the houses (100m), under the railway (Portsmouth line) and up to the T-junction (300m).

④ Go R to the road (150m) and up the footpath opposite to the field (150m). Cross the R corner into the next field (70m) then aim ½L, over the brow of the hill and down to the bottom corner near the house (250m). ❀ Cross the drive and go on along the bottom of the next field past the pond L (250m). Enton Hall is up R. Keep on ahead to the gate (100m), out of the field (40m) and fork R to the track junction (60m). ❀❋

⑤ Turn R along the path under trees. Carry on beside the Enton Hall grounds and through the car park to the road (500m).

⑥ Go L on the road (100m). After Sweetwater Pond take the winding path L through the wood. Avoid the L fork (150m) and carry on (350m) eventually beside a garden to the track from the house (100m). Turn L to the main road (150m) (King Edward's School, distant R). Cross and carry on along Combe Lane opposite (300m). ♣

⑦ Round the L bend, after one house take the footpath R over the railway and up beside the trees (200m). Stay ahead at the track junction to the house at the end of the track (400m) then on the footpath to the road at the hamlet of Sandhills (250m). Walk up the road L to the crossroads (250m).

⑧ Turn R up Sebastopol Lane to the next road (150m) then L up to the T-junction on top (200m). ★

ⓧ *Extension of 700m: Turn L (60m) and take the path R above the road. Keep close to the large field (Banacle Common), avoiding side paths L, around to the straight path between fields (700m).*

ⓨ *Turn R to Parsonage Farm Cottages (400m). Turn L ➧⑩*

⑨ Turn R along the road (150m) then diverge L beside the field on the path under trees (200m). At the track turn L down to Parsonage Farm Cottages (150m). Turn R.

⑩ Pass between the cottages (50m). Enter the field after the R garden and cross to the furthest corner (150m). Stay ahead over fields into the valley, down to the house (1000m) and past it on the drive up towards the road (200m).✱

⑪ At the bend just before the road, take the path ahead to the next drive (60m). Go down it R past the houses (100m) and continue down the steeper footpath ahead (300m).

⑫ Cross the drive and follow the path between gardens, round the pond and up the steps (100m) then L through the wood round the flank of the hill and up (200m). On top carry on along the path, or the lane beside it, to Witley Lodge (200m).

Witley Station at Wormley is on the Portsmouth Direct Line. The LSWR (London & SW Railway) opened to Woking in 1838 and had a branch line to Guildford by 1845. The tunnel under the North Downs extended the branch to Godalming in 1849 and also linked the two sections of the RGRR (Reading, Guildford & Redhill). The Woking branch line joined the LBSC Railway (London, Brighton & South Coast) at Havant which already ran trains to Portsmouth via Brighton. The new line provided a shorter route to Portsmouth from London so fights between railwaymen and companies broke out. The first legal scheduled direct train ran 21/1/1859. The route was electrified in 1937. The London terminus was originally at Nine Elms but had moved to Waterloo in 1848.

22 Witley, Hambledon and Wormley

About 8¼ km/5¼ miles; confusing heath and wood; undulating, half shady, good in winter. OS maps 1:25000 133 Haslemere, 1:50000 186 Aldershot.

Start at Witley Lodge, SU 945 396, near Witley Church or at Hambledon Church, SU 970 389m, or at the car park near Sweetwater Pond, SU 953 390.

The Merry Harriers ☎ 01428 682883
The White Hart ☎ 01428 683695

Linking walks
21❋ 23❊ 24❊ 28✦

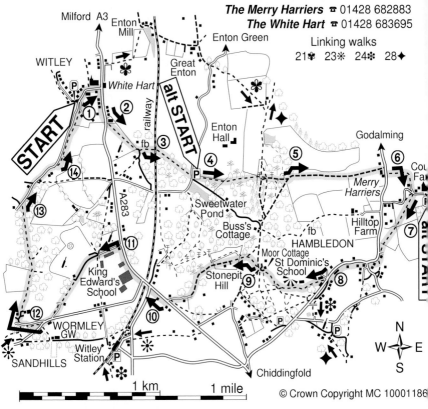

© Crown Copyright MC 10001186

① From Witley Lodge walk down the lane past Witley Church to the main road opposite the **White Hart** (200m) ❊ Turn R on the pavement down the main road (200m).

② Cross to the recreation ground beside Chichester Hall. Follow the L edge to the far corner (300m).

③ Join the track in the wood but almost immediately (30m) turn L down the footpath beside the garden, over the footbridge and under the railway (100m). Keep on to the road (300m).

④ Stay ahead over the road, past Sweetwater Pond car park, along the edge of the wood eventually to a broad cross track (500m) ✦ and on through the wood to the junction of broad bridleways (200m).

⑤ Turn L and follow the R bend (60m). Go on under trees between fields to the road in Hambledon next to the **Merry Harriers** (700m).

⑥ Over the road from the pub continue up the path and along the drive to the next road (300m). (Hambledon Church is 100m L).

⑦ Cross the road and climb the bank into the field. Go down the fields obliquely to the house (500m). Walk down the road past the side road L in the middle of the village (100m) and on to the gateway of St Dominic's School (300m). ✳

⑧ Diverge R up the path outside the school onto Hambledon Common. Disregard all L turns and keep on along the heath path round the flank of the hill to Moor Cottage (500m). ✳

⑨ Walk along the track from the house (30m). Turn R on the bridleway and immediately L steeply up to the top of Stonepit Hill (200m). Go through the gateway along the drive in front of the house (100m), and out down the drive to the A283 in Wormley (600m).

⑩ Cross to the pavement and follow the main road down R, over the railway (200m) and up past King Edward's School (300m).

⑪ After the school and houses turn L along the drive beside the sports field (200m). Stay ahead up the bridleway under trees, then a tarmac drive, to the next road (500m). Follow the road R (60m).

⑫ Over the brow of the hill, just after the side road (20m), turn R on the crossing path which is soon beside the side road. When the path ends, carry on along the side road to the trees (150m) and turn R on the first drive R. Continue on the path between gardens then through woodland. (The hill L is Bannicle Hill which had the semaphore tower on top). The path descends (500m) then rises to the next road (300m).

⑬ Follow the road R (300m).

⑭ Just after the large house, Hangerfield, watch out for a side path R. Follow it beside the lane down to the next house and keep on down the drive to the parking area at Witley Lodge (500m).

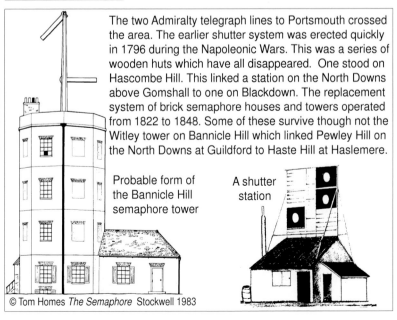

The two Admiralty telegraph lines to Portsmouth crossed the area. The earlier shutter system was erected quickly in 1796 during the Napoleonic Wars. This was a series of wooden huts which have all disappeared. One stood on Hascombe Hill. This linked a station on the North Downs above Gomshall to one on Blackdown. The replacement system of brick semaphore houses and towers operated from 1822 to 1848. Some of these survive though not the Witley tower on Bannicle Hill which linked Pewley Hill on the North Downs at Guildford to Haste Hill at Haslemere.

Probable form of the Bannicle Hill semaphore tower

A shutter station

© Tom Homes *The Semaphore* Stockwell 1983

23 Chiddingfold and Sandhills

About 9½ km/6 miles with an extension of 2 km/1¼ miles to Brook; undulating farmland and woodland mostly on the Wealden Clay; muddy in wet seasons; half shady. OS maps 1:25000 133 Haslemere, 1:50000 186 Aldershot.

Start from the bottom of Chiddingfold village green, SU 961 354. Witley Station has free parking at weekends. On the extension, park opposite the pub at Brook, SU 930 380.

Linking walks 18☆ 21✤ 22✳ 24◇ 25★ 26✳

① Cross Chiddingfold green to the corner of the garden wall halfway up the main road side (100m) and pass R of the pond (50m). Go R on the minor road (70m) and L on the track under trees (70m). Stay ahead up R of the graveyard and under the trees on the brow (250m), along the lane with houses to the bend (200m), between gardens (120m), along the top R edge of the field (450m) and between fences to houses (100m).

② Turn R to the field after the garden (50m). Cross obliquely and go along the top to the road (300m).

③ Go up the road R, over the rise (100m) and down to the T-junction (250m). Turn R to houses (350m).

④ Turn back on the track behind the 1st house L (100m). Go round the bend next to the drive and follow the yew hedge up the slope (300m), round a curve then level to the hedge bend R (200m). Stay ahead over the field (100m) into the wood, down into the valley to the brick bridge (150m), up the other side still in trees then outside fields R (250m), along the R edge of a field (150m), over the railway lines and the next field into trees (150m).

The Crown
☎ 01428 682255
The Swan
☎ 01428 684688
Dog & Pheasant
☎ 01428 682763
Winterton Arms
☎ 01428 682272

N
W—E
S

© Crown Copyright
MC 100011861

⑤ Follow the path down R (50m) and turn R along the valley (80m). Cross the bridge and go up to the side path L at the brow (150m).

ⓔ *Extension of 1¼ miles: Cross the footbridge L and carry on up through wood (100m) then field, R of the garden, to the road (400m). Almost opposite stay ahead up the path and track to the tarmac drive (200m). Drop L to the road (50m).*

(f) *Walk down the road L (200m). Turn R along the 2nd side path, at the garden hedge, and enter the cricket field at Brook (200m).* ☆

(g) *Cross to the top corner of the cricket field (200m). Go up through the trees (30m) then R along the hillside and L up to the field (200m).*

(h) *Turn R. Stay on this path (Greensand Way) round outside these fields to the road (550m).*

(i) *Go L to the junction (60m), R down Bannacle Hill Road (250m)* ✳ *and R down Sebastapol Lane to the crossroads (150m), then L.* ➔(7)

(6) Stay ahead up to fields (150m) then houses (400m) and up the vehicle track (50m). Opposite the diverging concrete drive L, turn into the field R and cross to the top gate at Sandhills (100m). ♣✳ Turn R.

(7) Walk down the road (200m). On the L curve after the house L, diverge R on the track beside the garden fence to a house L (250m). Stay ahead to the cross track (350m). Turn R (100m) Pass round the L bend to Witley Station and cross the footbridge (100m).

(8) Outside the station go R parallel with the railway through the car park and along the lane (150m). Turn L through the garden of Lilac Cottage. Stay ahead beside the wood to more houses, over the access road at the industrial estate (350m) and into a field (100m).

(9) Cross to the L corner (100m) then cross the road and the narrow field into Minepit Copse (40m). Follow the path through the trees and into a field (250m). Cross to the footbridge at the middle of the far side (200m). In the next field make for the far L corner (120m). Outside go L on the grass track (50m) and R up into the field.

(10) Aim out of the corner on the bisecting line and curve R round the slope down to the gateway (150m). Cross the narrow field and stream into the wood (30m) and go on up to more fields (150m). Go up the R edge (350m) and ahead to the road near the houses (150m).

(11) Walk down the road L (50m) Immediately after the side road L turn L on the path in the trees and descend to the field (150m). Cross to bottom corner (100m). ★

(12) Outside, cross the little stream and cross back R up the next field swinging L across to the corner R of the houses (200m). Continue on the track to the road (100m). Turn L on the pavement (50m) and R up Coxcombe Lane (100m).

(13) Take the path next to the house L on the crest of the rise. At the track keep on past the houses and cricket field to the A283 (250m).

(14) Follow the pavement R to the village green (200m) and cross to the bottom edge (100m). ✱

24 Hambledon Hurst and Chiddingfold

About 8½ km/5¼ miles with an extension of 1½ km/1 mile to Chiddingfold green; heath, wood and farmland, undulating. The Hurst tracks are very muddy in wet seasons. OS maps 1:25000 133 Haslemere, 1:50000 186 Aldershot.

Start from Hambledon cricket green, SU 963 380, where there are only a few parking places. At weekends parking is free at Witley Station. The extension has kerbside parking on the south side of Chiddingfold village green, SU 961 354.

Winterton Arms ☎ 01428 682272
The Crown ☎ 01428 682255
The Swan ☎ 01428 684688

Linking walks   21✳   22✻
23◆   25❂   26✳   28◆   35❂

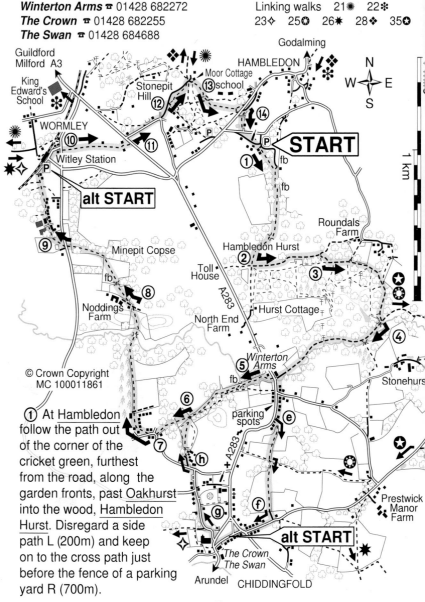

① At Hambledon follow the path out of the corner of the cricket green, furthest from the road, along the garden fronts, past Oakhurst into the wood, Hambledon Hurst. Disregard a side path L (200m) and keep on to the cross path just before the fence of a parking yard R (700m).

© Crown Copyright MC 100011861

48

② Turn L along the horse track. Watch out for the boundary mound beside it R (350m) and continue to the path junction after it (150m).

③ Fork R. Disregard the many side turns. The path passes fields (350m) then swings R down to the valley bottom (400m). ❍❍

④ Turn R over the horse bridge. Stay ahead along the valley, past the side bridge L (200m) to fields (450m) and on to the road at the **Winterton Arms** (300m).

ⓔ *Extension of 1½ km/1 mile to Chiddingfold village green: Go L on the pavement (300m). At the R curve take the path L up between gardens and along the L edge of the fields (300m). At the top turn L through the hedge then R beside it. Stay ahead to the road (400m).* ✳

ⓕ *Walk down the road (R), along the village green past the **Crown** and over to the* church *(450m).*

ⓖ *Go through the churchyard (100m), R to the far side (100m)* ✧ *and R to the road (70m). Follow the pavement to the end (400m).*

ⓗ *Turn L along the road (50m) then R on the track under trees (150m). Cross the field to the far end (200m). Enter the field L.* ✦⑥

⑤ Cross the road and take the path opposite the pub, over the stream (200m) and on under trees between fields (450m). At the little stream, cross into the R field.

⑥ Diverge from the L fence up to the middle of the far side (100m) and carry on up the path through the trees (150m).

⑦ Go R up the road (50m) then R up the path, past gardens (150m). Carry on at the L edge of the fields (350m), down through the wood (200m) and over the stream and narrow field (30m). Stay ahead up round the side of the L hillock into the top L corner (150m).

⑧ Outside turn L (50m) then cross the R field obliquely to the bend in the middle of the R edge (100m). Cross the footbridge. In the next field make for the far L corner (200m) then follow the path through Minepit Copse and over a strip of field to the road (300m).

⑨ Cross into the field opposite and aim obliquely into the trees at the protruding corner (100m). Continue between the industrial estate and houses (200m), along the edge of the wood and through the garden of Lilac Cottage to Witley Station (which is in Wormley) (250m). ✳❋

⑩ Follow the road R past the station and round to the T-junction (200m). Slightly R cross Combe Lane and take the path between gardens to the A283 (500m).

⑪ Cross slightly L (30m) and walk up Wormley Lane to the R bend (300m). Stay ahead up the sunken track between drives to the side path R next to the garden (100m).

⑫ Go up the side path (15m) then climb the steep bank L through the trees and follow the heath path above the sunken track. Rejoin the track before the house (250m). ❖

⑬ Walk down to the R corner of Moor Cottage, R past the garage and up the main path (200m). On top don't fork L but descend round the flank to Hambledon (300m).

⑭ Cross the road to the track from the house frontages below and turn R down the curving footpath to the village shop (150m) and cricket green.

25 Chiddingfold and Stonehurst

About 7 km/4½ miles with an extension of 1½ km/1mile; wood and farmland; undulating; half shady. The paths through the woods are unpleasant in wet seasons. OS maps 1:25000 133 Haslemere, 1:50000 186 Aldershot.

Start in Chiddingfold, parking at the bottom of the village green, SU 961 354.

Linking walks 23★ 24◐ 26✦ 35♣

Winterton Arms ☎ 01428 682272
The Crown ☎ 01428 682255
The Swan ☎ 01428 684688

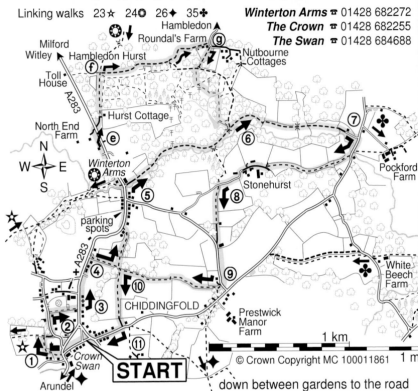

© Crown Copyright MC 100011861   1 m

★① At the corner of Chiddingfold green near the **Crown**, cross into the churchyard. Pass L of the church (100m) then turn R on the path across to the track (100m).

② Go R along the track (70m), L along the minor road (200m) and R through the recreation ground to the main road (200m). Cross.

③ Follow the pavement L, past the cricket field (200m) to the bent tarmac drive with path R (150m).

④ Go up the path (250m) and take the side path L across the field. Keep on at R edges then down between gardens to the road (300m). Follow the pavement R to the **Winterton Arms** (300m). ◐

ⓔ *Extension of 1½ km/1 mile in Hambledon Hurst: Continue on the L pavement up to the drive of North End Farm (450m) then cross the road and take the drive to Hurst Cottage (100m). Cross the grass in front of the house and go on into the wood to the cross path just after the parking yard L (250m).*

ⓕ *Turn R along the horse track. Watch out for the boundary mound R (350m) and continue to the path junction after it (150m). Fork L and*

50

keep on to the start of the road at Roundal's Farm (350m).

⑨ *Turn R beside the garden and keep on into the trees (150m). Cross the bridleway slightly R. Stay ahead on the smaller path, round a bend (100m), and over a crosspath (20m) to converge on a stream (120m). At the next cross path turn R over the stream to the fence above the pond (200m). Follow the fence down L to the bridleway T-junction at the foot of the slope (10m from a bridge R) (100m). Turn L.* ✦⑥

⑤ Turn R down the track between the bridge and pub. Stay ahead on the path beside fields (250m), into the wood, down the wooded valley (500m), past a side path R over the stream and a side path L 10m after a bridge (200m).

⑥ Carry on along the valley into fields (250m). Stay ahead near the L edges (350m). In the last field aim for the house beyond it (200m) and go out along the track past the house (100m). ✦

⑦ Turn back R along the road (150m). Just after the bridge and before the next house, turn off R along the path between fields (600m). At the top join the track skirting R of the Stonehurst Farm buildings (200m) and keep on round the S-bend and up the tarmac drive to the crossing path after the paddocks (200m).

⑧ Turn L into the field. Follow the L edge across it (250m) and continue down the track and along the road (L), rising to the next house R, Rystead (250m). ✦

⑨ Turn R across the drive, a little way into the trees (50m) then R

along the track to the fields. Go up the L edge (300m) then L into the adjacent field and on in the same direction at the R edge (400m).

⑩ At the end don't go on through the hedge but L round the corner. Stay ahead over the field and down the track to the road (400m).

⑪ Walk down the road R (250m) and along Chiddingfold green.

The English **glass-making industry** started around Chiddingfold. Glass beads appeared as early as 1500BC. in Egypt. Glass blowing first appears around 50BC in Palestine. In England the Romans and Saxons imported vessels and Bede writes of glazers coming from Gaul in the 7th century but the first known maker is Laurence, *Vitrearium*, de Dunkeshurstlonde (Duns Farm) who appears in a deed of 1226. His name also occurs in the accounts, supplying glass for the new Westminster Abbey in 1240. The early makers were all Flemish and French. The industry faded here after the use of timber was proscribed in 1620, but spread elsewhere under the same people. The Loseley Papers record a fracas between glass-makers in 1569 when a red hot glass-making rod found application.

Sand by itself melts at 1710°C to form silica glass but this temperature was beyond the first makers. Adding soda or potash (for sodium or potassium) formed silicate glass which melted at lower temperatures. Bracken ash was used locally for potash. A 2:1 mixture (by volume) of ash and sand was heated in stout clay pots in a wood fuelled furnace. The sand came from thin outcrops in the Weald Clay and from the Greensand; the terrain was dominated by woods coppiced for fuel. Later, window panes were cut from discs, up to 60 cm in diameter, made by fast spinning blown bulbs.

Wealden Glass 1226-1615 S E Winbolt 85p

26 Chiddingfold and Botany Bay Forest

About 7 km/4¼ miles with an extension of 3¾ km/2½ miles to the Sussex border. A Wealden Clay walk; avoid in wet seasons. Lots of shade for summer walking. Mostly level but with short steep slopes at the ghylls. Lots of stiles. OS maps 1:25000 133 Haslemere, 1:50000 186 Aldershot.

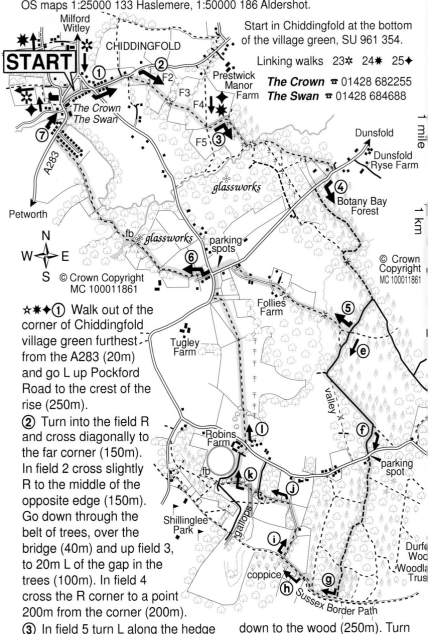

Start in Chiddingfold at the bottom of the village green, SU 961 354.

Linking walks 23✳ 24✳ 25✦

The Crown ☎ 01428 682255
The Swan ☎ 01428 684688

© Crown Copyright MC 100011861

© Crown Copyright MC 100011861

✭✳✦① Walk out of the corner of Chiddingfold village green furthest from the A283 (20m) and go L up Pockford Road to the crest of the rise (250m).

② Turn into the field R and cross diagonally to the far corner (150m). In field 2 cross slightly R to the middle of the opposite edge (150m). Go down through the belt of trees, over the bridge (40m) and up field 3, to 20m L of the gap in the trees (100m). In field 4 cross the R corner to a point 200m from the corner (200m).

③ In field 5 turn L along the hedge (150m). Go R round the corner and

down to the wood (250m). Turn L in the valley (20m) and cross the bridge. Go on along the valley (100m). Disregard the steep side path R. Stay ahead up through the wood to gardens (350m) and down beside fences to the road (200m).

④ Walk along the road R (200m) and turn L on the Botany Bay forest track. Follow it up to a broad curve (500m), round R then L, down over a bridge (200m) and up to a 3-way track junction (300m). Turn R on the hard track. Watch out for a crossing footpath (300m).

ⓔ *Extension of 3¾ km/2½ miles to the Sussex border: Stay on the track (300m), round a L bend on the edge of a valley and on (500m).*

ⓕ *Keep to the hard track when it bends ½R (200m). Cross the road and continue L of the house on the forest track (450m). At the unequal fork keep to the main track R, curving L, to the edge of the forest next to fields (550m).*

ⓖ *Turn R. Follow the boundary path past the ends of two fields L into the dip (250m).*

ⓗ *Don't go up to the R field but cross the boundary L (10m) and go on beside it (Sussex Border Path) over a rise to the end of the L fields (150m). Stay ahead briefly down beside chestnut coppice (60m) then turn R into the adjacent field.*

ⓘ *Cross the end of the field (200m) and go out down the drive from the house (200m).*

ⓙ *Turn L into the first field. Keep to the R edge (150m) and stay ahead R of the garden to the drive from the house (80m). Cross to the pond and pass R of it into the field (40m). Cross the gallops and follow the hedge to the end of the shallow R bulge (200m).*

ⓚ *Turn R through the hedge and cross to the track (40m). Follow the track R to Robins Farm (200m). Cross the track from the stables to pass R of the garden to the road (60m). Go L on the road (40m) and into the corner of the field R.*

ⓛ *Go up the field to the middle of the top edge (200m). Carry on at the L edge of the next field (500m). In the next field don't follow the edge but aim for the house at the middle of the top edge (300m). Cross into the narrow field and make for the far L corner (70m). Walk along the road R (150m). ➜⑥*

⑤ Turn R. Stay ahead past a path junction (50m), down to the stream, up to the edge of the forest, beside fields past Follies Farm L (550m) and along the drive (150m). When the drive bends L at barns, continue between hedges ahead and keep on to the road (150m). Turn L and walk along the R verge (200m).

⑥ At the road junction go up the tarmac drive to the garden gate (100m) and turn R through the hedge (10m). Go L round the fields, up, down, up to the wooded corner (500m). Go down through the trees and over foobridges at the pond (50m) then R up the stepped path to the field (80m). Carry on beside the wood (150m).

⑦ Before the end of the wood turn R down through the trees (50m). Continue on the path at the edge of the fields soon rising (200m). Just before the top of the L field drop down the bank R (10m) but continue in the same direction (100m) and pass behind gardens to the road (200m). Follow the road R to the Chiddingfold green (300m).

27 Hydon Heath and Tuesley

About 8½ km/5½ miles; farmland, heath and woods on the Greensand; half shady, short steep climbs. If starting from Ashstead Lane, a short cut of 1 km/¾ mile can be made and combined with the extension of ½ km/¼ mile. OS maps 1:25000 145 Guildford + 133 Haslemere 1:50000 186 Aldershot.

Start at Hydon's Ball car park, SU 978 402, or, on the extension, at the kerbside in Ashstead Lane, SU 968 425.

Linking walks
28☆ 31✳

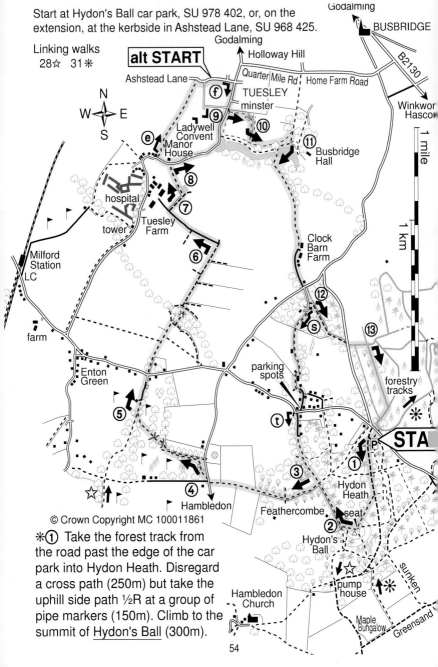

© Crown Copyright MC 100011861

✳① Take the forest track from the road past the edge of the car park into Hydon Heath. Disregard a cross path (250m) but take the uphill side path ½R at a group of pipe markers (150m). Climb to the summit of Hydon's Ball (300m).

54

② Turn R across the flat top away from the trig point and the Octavia Ball granite seat and drop to the path on the other side of the hill (100m). ☆ Go R, down beside the fence to the fence corner at the cross path (350m). Turn L.

③ Follow the path round the hillside, down beside coppice then between fields to the road (900m).

④ Slightly R take the path R of the track, ½R to the golf course. Pass between golf mounds and go on over the fairway into the trees (150m). Bear L along the fence to the corner of the field (200m). Don't continue ahead, but take the path ½R, through the belt of trees. Pass L of the mound, across a junction of golf tracks (100m) and obliquely over another fairway to the path in the trees (200m).

⑤ Go R to the house (60m). Stay ahead down the drive to the road (200m), along the path opposite beside the garden (100m) and over the field (Tuesley Fruit Farm) to the next trees (250m). Turn R (30m) then L through the trees and over the stream (100m). Turn L to the track junction (30m) then R (the original direction) on the field track to the major hard track L (500m).

⑥ Turn L towards the distant farm buildings (450m).

⑦ Before the sheds, turn R along the track at the edge of the field (150m) then L on the path beside the reservoir and down to the road at Tuesley Manor House (200m).

ⓔ *Extension of ½ km/¼ mile: Go L up the road (100m) and R on the path beside the next house. Cross a small valley and ascend between fields to the next road (600m).*

ⓕ *Go R on Ashstead Lane to the end (300m) then R down Tuesley Lane to the first field L (200m).* ➜⑨

⑧ Turn R. Follow the road down into the valley (400m) and up the other side to the field R (200m).

⑨ Go up the track into the field opposite the back gate of Ladywell Covent and L along the top edge to the shrine Tuesley Minster (100m). Go round the corner of the field down to the next corner (200m).

⑩ Turn L through the wood. Keep to the level paths above the steep slope then descend ahead to the sunken descending path (300m).

⑪ Go R down the sunken path, past Busbridge Lakes (exotic wild fowl) in the valley (200m), up to Clock Barn Farm (650m), along the drive to the road (250m) and along the drive opposite (150m).

ⓢ *Short cut of 1 km/¾ mile (minus Hydon's Ball): Fork L and take the path L after the house. Stay ahead at R edges to the shed. Go round it, R, L and ahead at L edges then along the drive to the road (800m).*

ⓣ *Turn R on the road (20m) then L up the drive past the houses (150m). Stay ahead up to the major cross path at a fence corner (350m). Turn R.* ➜③

⑫ Before the first house turn L on the bridleway and cross the road (400m). Go along the forestry track opposite (private tracks used by walkers). Disregard the path 1st R but turn at the track 2nd R (150m).

⑬ Follow this round a R bend (400m) and on to a broad U-bend L (200m). Watch out for a narrow side path R, halfway round the bend. Exit across the road into Hydon's Ball car park (50m).

28 Hydon's Ball to Hambledon

About 8 km/5 miles with a short cut of 1¾ km/1 mile. Heath and fields on the Greensand with good views. Good winter and summer; half shady, hilly. There are several places with confusing paths so allow time for getting lost. OS maps 1:25000 133 Haslemere +145 Guildford, 1:50000 186 Aldershot.

Start at Hydon's Ball National Trust car park, SU 978 402, or at Hambledon, SU 970 389, parking at the church (not Sundays) or at the *Merry Harriers*.

Linking walks 21✹ 22✦ 24❖ 27☆ 31✳ 33✿

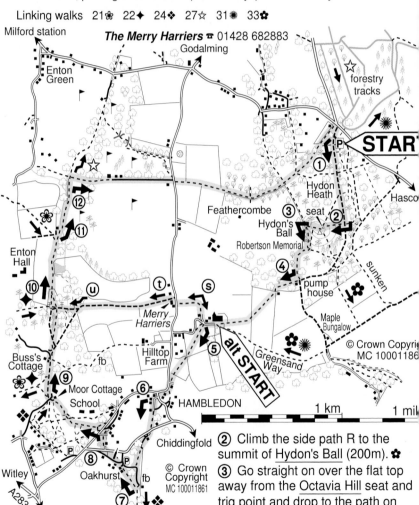

② Climb the side path R to the summit of Hydon's Ball (200m). ✿
③ Go straight on over the flat top away from the Octavia Hill seat and trig point and drop to the path on the other side (near fence) (100m). Descend L, past the memorial R to the cross path (150m). Turn R. The path curves L down to the pump-house (booster station - often concealed by vegetation) (250m).

✳① At Hydon Heath join the forest track from the road past the edge of the car park. Stay on it past a cross path with cairn (250m) up to the highest point (350m).

56

④ At the pumphouse junction take the path R to the fields (150m). Cross to Hambledon Church (600m). Go on along the lane past the church and Court Farm to the next house R (100m).

⑤ *Detour to pub or short cut of 1¾/1 mile: Turn R on the drive at the house and carry on down round to the* **Merry Harriers** *(300m). Return* →⑤ *or* ⓣ *Take the track R of the pub between fields (700m).*

ⓤ *After it bends into the wood (70m) fork R on the major branch track (200m) and turn R at the wide cross path.* →⑩

⑤ Don't go on down the lane but up the bank L into the field. Walk down the middle and out at the furthest corner. Keep on in the same line down to the house (500m). Go down the road (100m).

⑥ Turn L at the junction then fork R on the lane past the house fronts and go on down the path (250m). Over the road take the diverging path across the front of the house (300m). At the drive go L (100m).❖

⑦ At the next house L, turn back R past Oakhurst to the green (200m) and cross it obliquely to the shop (200m). Go up the path between pond and shop to the track with houses on top (200m).

⑧ Climb the grass bank L to the road and take the path opposite, up onto the Common. Stay ahead between the trees around the L side of the hill, past several side paths up and down the hill, to Moor Cottage (600m). ❀✦

⑨ After the house (50m) take the bridleway R along the foot of the slope. Disregard steep L branches and carry on down to Buss's

Cottage (300m). Don't continue on the drive but fork R. Disregard the 1st L back to the drive (40m) but bear L at the next fork to the cross path with overhead cables (300m).

⑩ Stay ahead to the field (100m), across to the corner of the wood (100m) and along the edge of the trees past the lake (250m).

⑪ Just before the track to the house, bear R (50m). Cross the brook and go up through the wood then up the L edge of the golf course to the cross track (350m). ☆

⑫ Turn R along the track past the club buildings (300m) to the road (400m). Cross to the track on the other side and carry on between fields (400m). Stay ahead up into the wood below Feathercombe on the hillside, past the fence corner at the downhill cross path from Hydon's Ball R (400m) to the 3-way split (100m). Take the middle path to the road next to Hydon's Ball car park (500m).

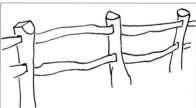

The rustic fences of W Surrey are cut from chestnut coppiced on a 30 year cycle. The posts are whole or ½ width logs, the rails ¼ or ⅛, split by hammer and chisel. Coppicing has survived because the steep Greensand slopes have little commercial use. In the past coppiced timber was used for making charcoal. John Evelyn estimated that Sussex had 200,000 acres of coppice in 1667, most of it used by iron works for smelting and forging. Coke was not used for smelting until 1707.

29 Thorncombe and Nurscombe

About 8 km/5 miles through tranquil Greensand country; hilly, in and out of the combes. The paths are well shaded. The views are better when the leaves are off the trees. OS maps 1:25000 145 Guildford, 1:50000 186 Aldershot.

There is no large parking place. Start in Thorncombe Street layby, SU 999 421.

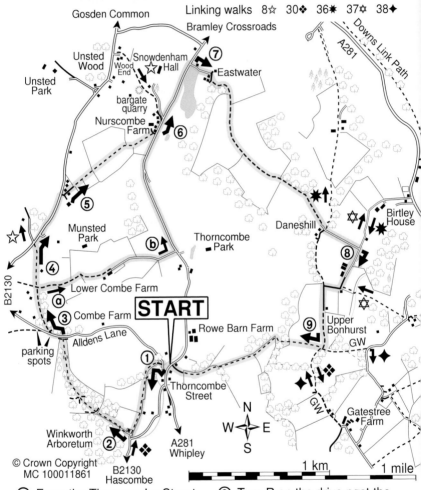

① From the Thorncombe Street layby go down the road (60m) and take the 1st R (70m). Cross the bridge then turn L on the track in the trees (50m) and skirt L round the bottom edge of the fields (600m). At the end, stay ahead across the L end of the garden of Phillimore Cottage (20m).

② Turn R on the drive past the cottage (30m) and continue on the footpath and R into the field (40m). Follow the edge L rising to the wood (200m). Stay ahead on the path up the R side of the coomb (350m), over the Bargate rock on the edge of the plateau and along the top to the road (250m).

③ Walk up the road L (100m) and take the bridleway R, below the garden, round the top of the field to the 4-way path junction (300m).

ⓐ *Alternative ½ km/¼ mile longer: Take the path R between the fields down the ridge past Lower Combe Farm (500m) and continue down the drive (500m).*

ⓑ *At the bottom follow the road L to Nurscombe Farm (800m).* ➜⑥

④ Keep on down the path ahead (300m) ☆ then R down the road past the drive of Munstead Park to the next houses R (400m).

⑤ Turn R into the shared drive. Go round the bend and on past all the houses then between fields, eventually descending into the combe. Join the road outside Nurscombe Farm (800m). Turn L.

⑥ Stay on the road, past the houses, down to the end of the large pond R (500m). The large house up L is Snowdenham Hall.

⑦ Turn R along the Eastwater drive. When it bends to the house (150m) take the track R round the barns (70m) and L up out of the combe, then between fields up to the house Daneshill (1300m). ✳ Carry on straight down the drive to the T-junction (300m). ✿

⑧ Turn R up the farm drive. Keep on past the barns to the house L (300m), round the R bend in the track to the top (100m) and L to Upper Bonhurst (200m). Stay ahead along the bridleway to the staggered cross track (250m). ❖✦

⑨ Turn R into the field and go straight up the spur of the ridge into the trees (200m). Follow the footpath up round bends R & L to the top (150m) then at R edges up

to and over the flat top field (350m) and down the other side. Descend at the edge of the grass rather than in the sunken path but keep watch on the path to cross the fence near the bottom (200m). Carry on down and out beside the house to the road in Thorncombe Street (150m).

A **combe** or coomb is a valley set in a hillside. The word, a Celtic remnant, is part of *Comp*ton and Welsh place names with *Cwm*. Here, Nurscombe, Thorncombe, Hascombe, Binscombe and Farncombe lie below the plateau of the calcareous Bargate sandstone. As it overlies softer Lower Greensand strata the escarpment and valleys are steep and calcium improves the soils below. Bargate is the pleasant brown stone of the old houses in the district. The origin of the name is unknown

The Greensand follows the lie of the chalk all around the Weald but only in this area does it have Bargate. The best quarries on the valleysides over Godalming yielded large blocks called *doggers* that were split for building, sometimes to mimic bricks. Another peculiarity of the Godalming district is the galetting of Bargate walls where small ironstone chips are inserted in the pointing to protect the mortar.

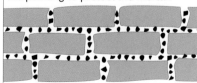

Further from Godalming, the stratum is composed of smaller stones as seen in craggy roadsides. In walls, it is uncut, irregular and more crumbly.

The use of stone declined around the time lorries arrived; so, if ordinary garden walls are stone, it must have been available close by and easy to obtain. Some of the hillsides will have been scarped by stone collectors.

30 Winkworth and Thorncombe Street

About 8½ km/5¼ miles with an extension of 1½ km/1 mile; hilly farmland and bluebell woods on the Lower Greensand. In Winkworth Arboretum you should keep to the public footpath unless you are a National Trust member or have paid. OS maps 1:25000 145 Guildford, 1:50000 186 Aldershot.

The best place to start is the car park of Winkworth Arboretum (10am opening), on the B2130, SU 989 412. This used to be free but now is only for NT members and paying visitors. On the route is a layby in Thorncombe Street, SU 999 421. On the extension, start from the parking area opposite the *White Horse* in Hascombe, TQ 001 394.

Linking 29❖ 31✪ 32✿ 34✳ 36✱ 37★ 38✪

The White Horse
☎ 01483 208258
Winkworth Arboretum NT
☎ 01483 208477

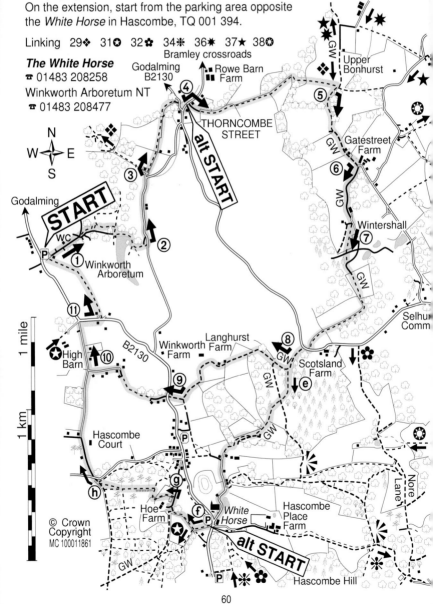

© Crown Copyright
MC 100011861

① At the innermost corner of the car park take the public footpath into Winkworth Arboretum L of the house (250m). At the 3-way split go down the stepped middle path. Stay on the public footpath down the R side of the little coomb to the bottom (300m), R to the pond (40m) and L along the end of it. Keep on to the road (300m).

② Walk along the road L to the drive up L on the R bend (450m).

③ Go up the drive of Phillimore Cottage (50m). ❖ Turn back R and take the path R of the garage. Stay ahead at the R edge of the fields (550m). From the 3rd field, exit at the gate R to the road in Thorncombe Street (50m).

④ Go R to the junction (70m) then L (70m). Turn up the track beside the house R and continue up the L edge of the fields over the top and into the wood (800m). Descend to the next field (150m) and straight down the spur of the hill to the track junction immediately outside the bottom hedge (200m). ✸★

⑤ Turn R up the Greensand Way horse track. Keep on below the hill to the gateway of Gatestreet Farm at the tarmac lane (600m). ✪

⑥ Turn R along the track in the field round the L edge. Stay ahead to the house drive R (400m).

⑦ Diverge R up the grass, skirting the garden of Wintershall L into the trees (200m). Cross the uphill track and carry on to join the next track up out of the little valley (150m). Cross the top of the next field (200m) and continue through the wood round outside fields to the road (600m). ✿ Turn R to the bend (70m) and L up the track (200m). ✪

ⓔ *Extension of 1½ km/1 mile to Hascombe and the White Horse: At the R bend in the main track, go up the track ahead, over a cross track (GW) (200m) and past a shed L (300m). From the track diverge R on the path down to the lane between houses (250m). Carry on ahead, around the pond and past the church to the pub (500m).* ✳

ⓕ *Cross one field opposite the* **White Horse** *(150m). Don't stay on the GW ✪ but turn R on the path between the fields into the trees (200m). At the end fork down R to the wall (25m) and go R down the drive from Hoe Farm (80m).*

ⓖ *Turn L up into the field and go up the L edge to the top corner (150m). In the next field turn R immediately up through the wood (100m). On the bank (lynchet?) take the first side path L (250m). After a side track L, fork R (150m) then join the road R (30m).*

ⓗ *Cross and carry on ahead up past Hascombe Court (300m) and on along the lane (450m).* ♦⑩

⑧ Go round the R bend and up steeply, passing a side track L on top (150m). Go on down between fields past two houses (350m), winding gently downwards to the 3-way junction (450m).

⑨ Take the bridleway R towards the house (150m). Cross the main road and go up the steep track to the top (400m) then follow the lane L to the T-junction (200m). Turn R.

⑩ Keep on to the road (300m).

⑪ Turn R along the main road (150m). Just over the brow of the hill, between drives, turn off L on the footpath outside Winkworth Arboretum to the car park (600m).

31 Hydon's Ball and Hascombe

About 8½ km/5¼ miles with an extension of 1¼ km/¾ mile; heath and farmland on the Lower Greensand; hilly with good views. Good in winter but muddy; soft sand in summer. OS maps 1:25000 133+134+145, 1:50000 186 Aldershot.

Start at Hydon's Ball NT car park on Salt Lane, SU 979 402, or at Hascombe, parking opposite the *White Horse*, TQ 001 394.

Linking 27✳ 28✳ 30✪ 32✳ 33✳ 34✳

The White Horse
☎ 01483 208258

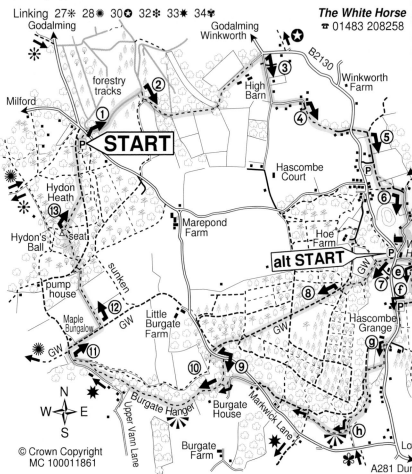

© Crown Copyright
MC 100011861

① Within Hydon's Ball car park look for the footpath to the road and cross into the forest (80m). Go R on the forestry track until the track bends L into a valley (550m).
② Take the path R. Disregard the side path R (80m) and stay ahead up under trees all the way to the houses and main road (1100m). ✪

③ Don't join the road but turn back R on the narrow lane (350m) and take the first side lane L (250m).
④ At the end go round the bend R beside the wall and down to the main road (400m). Follow the path opposite to the T-junction (100m)
⑤ Turn R. Stay ahead on the track beside fields and past a house

62

(300m). Cut the corner L over the fields or keep on round the L bend (100m) to the house (200m). ✽

⑥ Turn R on the lane, winding round the pond and Hascombe Church to the road junction at the *White Horse* (500m). ✽

ⓔ *Extension of 1¼ km/¾ mile: Go up the drive beside the pub (100m) and R on the path beside the shed after the house. Climb the R bank and follow the parallel track (250m).*

ⓕ *Turn down the 1st track R to the road (at the car park). Go L on the road to the house drive L (250m).*

ⓖ *Opposite it, take the path R up into the field. Continue above the road (150m) then cross to the top of the fields (150m). Turn L on the track (50m). When it bends uphill, stay ahead into the wood (350m).*

ⓗ *After the houses bear L down the slope beside the fence (100m) and turn R on the level path above the field (300m).✱ At the end turn R up to the track (50m) and follow it L to the end at the road (400m). Cross to Burgate Lodge and follow the drive diverging from the road (150m). After the L bend (50m) turn R over the grass up to the path in the wood (50m). Turn L.* ➜⑩

⑦ Take the Greensand Way path across the field opposite the pub, over a cross path and up the next field into the wood (250m). Bear R steeply up the flank of the hill to the junction on the top brow (150m).

⑧ Turn R to join the adjacent uphill path (20m). Follow that L across the flat hilltop (GW) (800m) and down to the road (200m).

⑨ Turn L down the road (100m) and take the next path R (150m).

⑩ Stay on the path along the foot of the hanger past Burgate House (100m) until near the lane (800m). Either join the lane or fork R up to the edge of the field but keep on ahead to the track junction near Maple Bungalow (300m). ❀

⑪ Turn R along the broad sandy track between fields (GW) (300m).

⑫ Take the 1st L between fields which curves R at trees to a cross track (400m). Don't turn here but cross up to the next track (10m) then turn R (50m), L (30m) and R to the top of Hydon's Ball (200m). ✳

⑬ Behind the Octavia Hill seat bear R down to the track (300m). Descend L to the car park (350m).

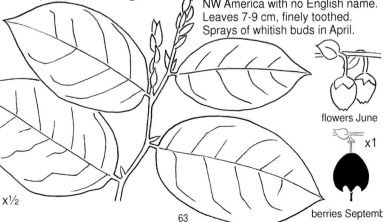

Gaultheria shallon on Hydon's Ball is a giant cousin of bilberry from NW America with no English name. Leaves 7-9 cm, finely toothed. Sprays of whitish buds in April.

flowers June

x1

x½

berries Septemb

32 Hascombe Hill and Scotsland Farm

About 7 km/4½ miles with a short cut of 2¼ km/1½ miles; woods and fields on the Greensand; good views; shady; hilly. In wet seasons the horse tracks become very muddy. OS maps 1:25000 133+134+145, 1:50000 186 Aldershot.

Start at Hascombe. Park opposite the *White Horse*, TQ 001 394.

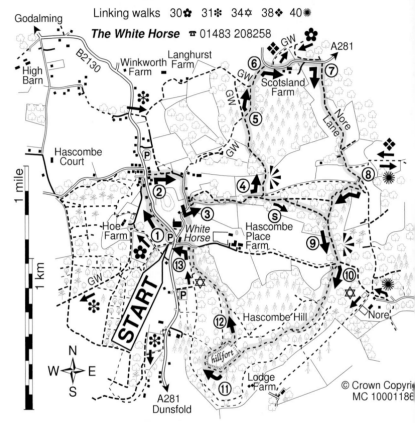

Linking walks 30✿ 31✽ 34✿ 38❖ 40✺

The White Horse ☎ 01483 208258

✿✽① Opposite the **White Horse** join the path outside the field and follow it with the road into Hascombe to the fountain (500m).

② Opposite the fountain go along the footpath between the gardens, over the millstream and up the wider track to the lane (250m). Go R along the tarmac lane until it bends R (200m).

③ Turn L into the steep drive and take the bridleway beside it up the hillside. The footpath R cuts two

corners and re-joins later. Carry on to the highest point beside the fields L (600m).

Ⓢ *Short cut of 2¼ km/1½ mile: Keep on through the wood (150m) then fork R to the junction on the edge of the hill (300m). Turn R.* →⑨

④ Take the side path L along the ridge between fields (Gatwick Airport visible R in the distance) (150m). Go on through the wood past a field corner (200m) and down to the crossing track (200m).

64

⑤ Turn R and stay ahead down to the road (400m). ❖

⑥ Follow the road R, down past Scotsland Farm, up over the rise (200m) and down to the bottom of the first field (200m).

⑦ Turn R up the track below the fields (Nore Lane). Pass over a rise (500m), down to the pond R in the dip (sometimes dry) (200m) ✷ and on up to the sunken part under the end of the next field R (200m).

⑧ Climb the stepped path R to the top of the bank (10m) but don't go R up the edge of the field. Instead follow the path L along the top of the bank (50m) then turn R up the horse track. After a steep winding portion it bends L to the top (250m). Disregard the side track R here and the next (150m).

⑨ Carry on along the ridge track down to a 4-way junction (300m). ✿

⑩ Take the oblique uphill path, which joins another (50m), up Hascombe Hill. Disregard the diverging path R (150m) and go on along the level path at the S (L) edge of the ridge. Pass a downhill path back L (300m) and the corner of the hill fort R (400m) and keep on to the end of the ridge (200m).

⑪ Follow the path as it bends R round the end of the hill (100m) then curves back along the other side (250m). Another R bend brings you to a path junction at the next corner of the hillfort (20m).

⑫ Turn L along the hill but diverge immediately on the main downhill path. Stay ahead down to the sunken path along the foot of the hill (550m) then bear R to the end near a house L (100m).

⑬ Go L down the tarmac drive to the *White Horse* (100m).

Hascombe Hill and Gibbet Hill are largely composed of Hythe Sands, the Greensand stratum below the Bargate beds, seams of jointed grey stone with sand between. Further east Leith Hill is part of the same outcrop on the north edge of the Weald. The strata were domed as a ripple in the earth's crust by the colliding African and Eurasian tectonic plates which pushed up the Alps. Erosion has removed the chalk and sand in the middle leaving rough edges.

The Hythe Sands lack calcium and do not retain water so they are covered by heath on hilltops where drainage is greatest. On the northern slopes of the hills the fields are on the calcareous Bargate sandstone and the transition from grey (Hythe) to brown (Bargate) sand or stone is visible in worn paths.

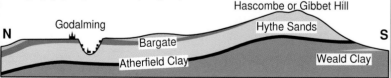

The lowest division of the Lower Greensand is the Atherfield Clay. It is not hard and does not stand out in valley sides but it causes the springs on the hillsides as water from the sand leaks over its edges. It forms dense clay soils which do not sustain arable agriculture because oxygen cannot move to the roots and microbes. Where the sand from the hills mixes with the clay the soil can be very fertile, hence the wheat fields south of the hills.

Greensand is misleading. It was a working title of early geologists for a series of predominantly sand layers, rarely green and with clays part of the series.

33 Dunsfold and Burgate Farm

About 7½ km/4½ miles with a hilly extension of 3 km/2 miles; farmland and woods on the Greensand and Weald Clay; good for spring flowers; half shady. OS maps 1:25000 133 Haslemere + 134 Crawley, 1:50000 186 Aldershot.

Start at Dunsfold, TQ 006 363, from the car park on the village green.

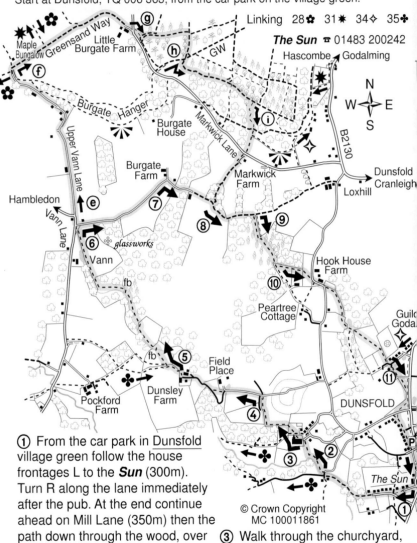

Linking 28 ✿ 31 ✳ 34 ◇ 35 ✤

The Sun ☎ 01483 200242

© Crown Copyright
MC 100011861

① From the car park in Dunsfold village green follow the house frontages L to the *Sun* (300m). Turn R along the lane immediately after the pub. At the end continue ahead on Mill Lane (350m) then the path down through the wood, over the stream (250m) and on to the next house (150m). ✤✤

② Turn R across the bridge (20m) then take the footpath L beside the stream to the well and on up to Dunsfold Church (250m).

③ Walk through the churchyard, round the church (100m) and up R to the adjacent small field. Cross it to the top L corner (100m). Pass into the next field and follow the L edge to the corner (150m), then up R to the tarmac drive (200m).

66

The wooded ridge ahead is the Lower Greensand escarpment, Holloways Heath L and Hascombe Hill R.

④ Turn L along the drive to Field Place (300m) and descend to the valley bottom either straight down the field or down the track L and round the hairpin bend (300m). Follow the track up the other side to Dunsley Farm (150m).

⑤ Next to the top barn, turn R on the side path to the fence (50m). Go round the field to the gateway R (100m) and into the field below. Don't follow the path along the hedge but go straight down the field to the bottom L corner (150m) and out over the footbridge. Follow the path L along the bottom of the fields (300m), through the wood near the stream, across the foot-bridge (250m) and up the valley side to the field (250m). Keep on along the L edge past the house, Vann, to the road (350m).

ⓔ *Extension of 3 km/2 miles: Stay ahead up Upper Vann Lane curving past houses (700m) to the sandy track on top (500m).* ✿

ⓕ *Turn R along the cart track (Greensand Way) in front of Maple Bungalow.* ✴ *Keep on over the rise and round down through Little Burgate Farm to the road (1100m).*

ⓖ *Cross to the path in the trees. Ascend beside the road (60m) then turn up the path L. Don't follow the L bend but keep on up the cleft to the almost level cross track (350m).*

ⓗ *Turn R and cross the GW on the brow of the hill (150m). Keep on opposite (80m). The path bends L to follow the edge of the hill. Look for the Break Neck path over the edge opposite the curving side*

path L (350m) but stay ahead watching out for the next path over the edge (50m before the next major side track L) (200m).

ⓘ *Turn R here and drop down the steep winding path (200m). Cross the forest track to the field (50m)* ✦ *and go down the edge to the road (150m). Carry on opposite, past the wall of Markwick Farm and down the field track to the T-junction in the trees (400m). Turn L.* ➔⑧

⑥ Turn R along the tarmac drive to Burgate Farm (700m).

⑦ At the junction near the house take the tarmac drive R to the barn R (200m) and carry on along farm track past a side track L at the double bend (200m). ✦

⑧ Stay on the track to the side path R near the end of the next block of woodland R (350m).

⑨ Follow this path down through the trees, past the corner of a field L (150m) and on to the corner of another field (200m).

⑩ Go L along the edge of the fields (200m) and ½R over the field before Hook Farm to the road (100m). Go round the L bend in the road to the R bend (80m) then into the L field. Cross the end to the wood and follow the edge round into the dip L (250m). Go down the path under the trees past the pond and up to the next field (50m). Cross over the rise obliquely to the far L corner (250m). Go on along the L hedge past the next field (100m) and out L to the pond and village green at Dunsfold.

⑪ Follow the path R round the edge of the green to the side road (450m). Cross and go on along the frontages to the car park (200m).

34 Hascombe and Dunsfold

About 8½ km/5¼ miles with an extension of 2 km/1¼ miles; some steep paths, numerous stiles, fine views, soft sand in summer, half shady, bad mud in wet seasons. OS maps 1:25000 133 + 134 + 145, 1:50000 186 Aldershot.

Start from Hascombe at the parking area opposite the *White Horse*, TQ 001 394, or, on the extension, from Dunsfold village green car park, TQ 006 363.

Linking walks 30✳ 32✿ 31✾ 33◇ 35★ 40❀

The White Horse ☎ 01483 208258   **The Sun** ☎ 01483 200242

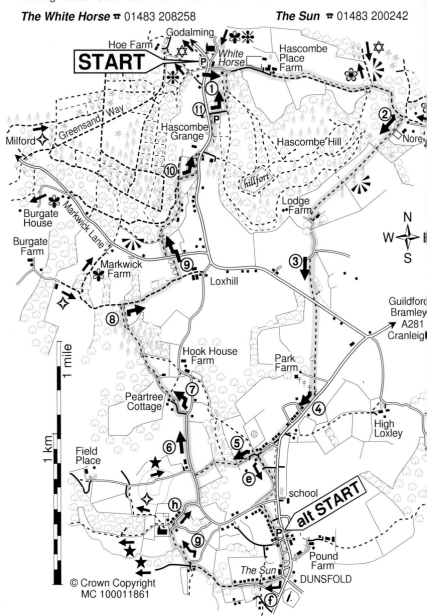

© Crown Copyright
MC 100011861

✳✿① Go up the drive beside the **White Horse** past a house and side path R (100m). Stay ahead onto the ridge. After Hascombe Place Farm the path in the L field is nicer than the track (1100m). ❀ On the ridge, admire the view

> The great valley below is aligned with the notch where the Wey cuts through the North Downs at Guildford. It would have been carved by the Ice Age river. In it are Cranleigh Water, the Junction Canal, the Horsham road and railway.

then carry on down steeply to the L bend at the next house (300m).

② Take the path up R beside the garden, through the wood, along the fields parallel with the top edge and down past the shed (1000m). Continue down the drive (200m).

③ Turn R on the lane (40m) and L into the field L. Descend, R of the ponds, to the (nasty) road crossing (300m). Continue down the fields, past the lone tree, over the drive and, in the same oblique line, to the trees L, 100m before the houses (600m). Join the road.

④ Walk along the verge R to the bend (350m) then cut the corner R and follow the lane past the ponds at the end of Dunsfold village green into the corner (200m).

ⓔ *Extension of 2 km/1¼ mile: Go L round the corner and keep to the path at the R edge (450m). Cross the next lane and follow the house frontages past the car park L (200m) to the **Sun** (300m).*

ⓕ *Turn R along the lane after the pub. At the end continue ahead on Mill Lane (350m) and down the path through the wood, over the bridge (250m) and on to the house L (150m). ★★*

ⓖ *Cross the bridge R (20m) and take the footpath L beside the stream to the well then R up to Dunsfold Church (250m). ✧ Walk round the church and back out.*

ⓗ *Depart along the upper lane (300m). At the T-junction turn L along the lane (200m).* ➔⑥

⑤ Go into the field and along the track at the L edge. Stay ahead down into the wooded valley, up to the next field and ahead at the R edge to the road (450m). Turn R.

⑥ Pass the drive of Field Place L and stay on the road to the next drive L (400m).

⑦ Go up the drive to Pear Tree Cottage and skirt the lawn to enter the field R of the house (100m). Follow the L edge of the fields (400m). Stay ahead through the wood and along the L edge of the next field to the track (400m). ❀

⑧ Go R along the track to a line of trees L before the buildings (450m).

⑨ Take the footpath L across the field (150m). Turn L up the road (30m) then R up the hill (200m). Avoid side paths at the top of the fields. Go on up through the trees, round R (50m) and along the contour path above houses then down the edge of the trees (350m).

⑩ After the descending track L (50m), turn R down the path beside the paddock (150m) and go along the bottom of the field to the road (100m). Go L on the road (250m).

⑪ Turn R on the track at the car park (150m) and L on the track along the foot of Hascombe Hill (250m). Just before the house, join the sunken path R. Go L to the drive (50m) and descend L to the *White Horse* (100m).

35 Dunsfold and Pockford

About 7½ km/4½ miles; an undulating Weald Clay walk through farmland and woods; muddy in wet seasons; excellent for bluebells and other spring flowers. OS maps 1:25000 133 Haslemere +134 Crawley, 1:50000 186 Aldershot.

Start from Dunsfold, TQ 006 363, at the little car park on the village green.

Linking walks 24✪ 25✪ 33✤ 34★   *The Sun* ☎ 01483 200242

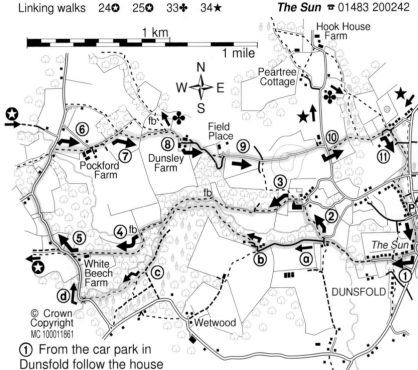

© Crown Copyright
MC 100011861

① From the car park in Dunsfold follow the house frontages L to the **Sun** (300m). Turn R along the road after the pub. At the end continue on the path, then along Mill Lane (350m). Keep on down the track through the wood, over the bridge (250m) and on to the house L (150m).

ⓐ *Slightly longer alternative, muddy in wet seasons: Cross the drive and go straight on up the track beside the wood (450m).*

ⓑ *At the path junction just after the cottage turn R & L & R on the main track to the next cottage (100m). Just before the garden take the footpath R into the valley*

(600m). At a L bend in the stream join the forestry track and follow it R near the stream until it bends L up the valley side (300m).

ⓒ *Take the side path up ahead (100m) then the lesser path down R. Follow the stream all the way to the next road (400m).*

ⓓ *Go over the bridge and up the road to White Beech (400m).* ➤**⑤**

② Cross the bridge R (20m) and take the path L beside the stream to the well then R up into Dunsfold Churchyard (250m). Walk round the church and up R into the adjacent small field (100m).

③ Go L along the edge (60m), down the edge of the next field (100m) and through the wood at the edge (150m). At the track turn into the field and follow the edge R (200m). When the field bends R go straight over to the L corner, near the stream (100m), over the bridge, through the wood (400m) and on beside the next field (200m).

④ At the end of the field bear L over the footbridge and climb out of the valley (100m). Keep on along the path to the road at White Beech Farm (600m). ✪ Turn R.

⑤ Stay on the road, over the hill and down to the junction (550m). Carry on R down Vann Lane to the bridge just after Rosebank Cottage (300m).

⑥ Immediately after the bridge cross the field R to the gate near the barns of Pockford Farm (250m) (or stay on the road (200m) and take the farm drive R (250m) then L). Follow the track past the buildings to the fields (100m). When it bends R keep on in the field ahead along the edge (150m).

⑦ Halfway along the small wood, L, join the crossing path ½R up the field (150m). Go through the hedge and on along the L edge of the next field (300m). ♣ The hedge curves up R to a barn and is joined by paths at the gap L.

⑧ Before the barn, the path diverges L through the hedge to Duns Farm (50m). Walk down the track (L) between the buildings into the valley (200m) and up the other side. Keep on the track up round the hairpin bend (300m) or cut the corner straight up the steep field to the drive from Field Place.

⑨ Continue on the drive, over the rise and down to the road (800m).★

⑩ Go along the road R (50m) and into the field opposite. Follow the L edge to the end (150m). Keep on down through the trees, up the other side (150m) and along the R edge of the next field to the corner of the green at Dunsfold (150m).

⑪ Follow the R edge of the green round to the side road (450m). Cross it and carry on along the frontages to the car park (200m).

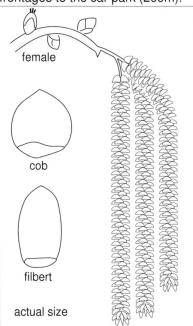

female

cob

filbert

actual size

Hazel catkins are male inflorescences with hundreds of small flowers which shed pollen before the leaves unfurl. As they use the wind for pollination they do not need colourful flowers to attract insects. The female flowers cluster inside a bud with only stigmas protruding to catch the pollen. Cobs are the fruits of a cultivar of the native hazel, *Corylus avellana*. The longer filbert is *C. maxima*, from S Europe, but cultivated in Britain. Quantities of nuts are excavated in stone age sites.

36 Bramley and Lordshill

About 9 km/5½ miles; undulating farmland on the Lower Greensand and the villages with a steeper extension of 3 km/1¾ mile over Chinthurst Hill; fairly shady. OS maps 1:25000 145 Guildford, 1:50000 186 Aldershot.

Start in Bramley; park at the disused railway station, TQ 010 451, or around the village hall in Hall Road. On the extension start from Chinthurst Hill car park.

Linking 9✿ 11✦ 29✳ 30✳ 37✿ ㉕ ★ ㉜ ✳

The Grantley Arms ☎ 01483 893351
The Wheatsheaf ☎ 01483 892722
The Jolly Farmer ☎ 01483 893355

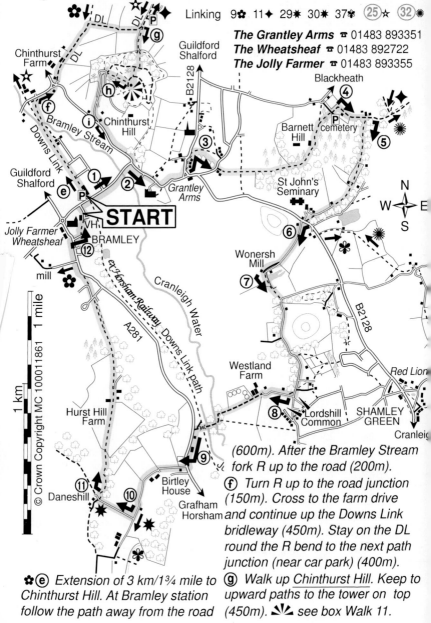

✿ⓔ Extension of 3 km/1¾ mile to Chinthurst Hill. At Bramley station follow the path away from the road (600m). After the Bramley Stream fork R up to the road (200m).

ⓕ Turn R up to the road junction (150m). Cross to the farm drive and continue up the Downs Link bridleway (450m). Stay on the DL round the R bend to the next path junction (near car park) (400m).

ⓖ Walk up Chinthurst Hill. Keep to upward paths to the tower on top (450m). ◥◣ see box Walk 11.

72

ⓗ *Behind the tower (opposite the doorway) find the steepest path. Descend (200m) and go down the tarmac drive to the road (350m).*

ⓘ *Walk down the road L to the next junction (350m) then L.* ➜②

✿① From Bramley Station follow the road away from the village centre over the Bramley Stream and round the R bend (400m). ✦

② Keep on past Wonersh church and along The Street to the Pepper Pot and ***Grantley Arms*** (450m).

③ Turn L towards Guildford. Walk on the grass by the gardens R of the road (150m). When the green widens, follow the R edge round to the next road (150m). Cross slightly R (30m) to the track at the timber-framed house. Go up the path between fields and over Barnett Hill (700m). After the eponymous house (150m) fork R down to the track (100m) and go on past the cemetery to the bend (70m).

④ Go round the R bend and down the sunken track (200m). ✳

⑤ Opposite the houses turn R on the path down the valley. Pass through small fields and a garden (450m) and on (200m). After the next house continue down the tarmac drive to the R curve (350m) then take the path ahead to the main road (nasty exit) (100m). ❁

⑥ Cross slightly R and go down the drive of Wonersh Mill house (350m). Fork R on the parallel track R of the garden (100m).

⑦ Turn L beside the garden wall over the millstream. Go on along the track (200m) then along the road (R) past the knoll L (700m).

⑧ Just before the side road L, where the trees give way to grass at Lordshill Common, turn R along the tarmac drive to Westland Farm (150m). Skirt the buildings and carry on along the track (450m), round bends over Cranleigh Water and the Junction Canal, under the Downs Link (ex-Horsham Railway) and up to the A281 (300m).

⑨ Follow the pavement down L (300m). On the curve cross to the first drive opposite. Go up it past Birtley House and on (550m). ✳

⑩ Before the farm buildings turn R up the tarmac drive (300m).

⑪ Just before the house take the path R in the trees then between fields to Hurst Hill Farm (700m). Keep on through the woods down to Bramley (700m), ahead on the road (100m) then between houses (100m) and along the A281 (250m).

⑫ Before the ***Wheatsheaf*** and ***Jolly Farmer*** turn R on Windrush Close (60m) and L on the footpath. Continue past the village hall to the road (200m) then R (100m).

The **River Wey** appears to have had its original channel through Bramley for the hills are the sides of a great valley aligned with the notch where the river cuts through the Downs at Guildford. The rivulet in the valley is called Bramley Stream and Cranleigh Water. It flows into the present Wey at Shalford just above the Tilling Bourne.

The Wey starts as two rivers, each called Wey, which rise near Alton and Churt. They join at Tilford and flow to the Thames at Weybridge.

The murky streams in the clay clefts around Dunsfold and Chiddingfold flow the other way. They are the headwaters of the Arun which they join via the Loxford Stream. The Arun rises near Horsham and empties into the English Channel at Littlehampton.

37 Shamley Green to Daneshill

About 7 km/4½ miles with an extension of 2km/1¼ mile: on the Lower Greensand across the great Wey valley mainly through arable farmland. OS maps 1:25000 145 Guildford, 1:50000 186 Aldershot.

Start from Shamley Green, parking at the roadside in Woodhill Lane near the pond, TQ 032 438, or, when there is no cricket, at the Arbuthnot Hall. On the extension start at the Run Common layby, TQ 032 419.

Linking walks 29✿ 30★ 36❀
38◇ 39✿ (32)◆ (33)◆

Red Lion
☎ 01483 892202
Bricklayers Arms
☎ 01483 898377

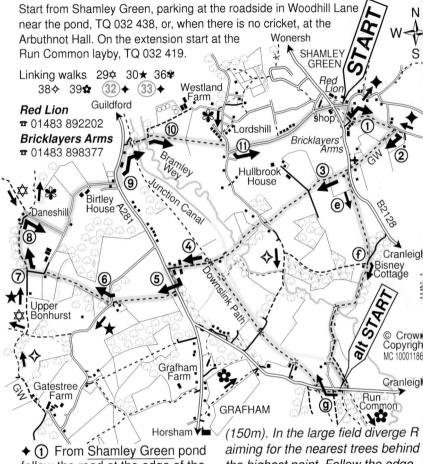

◆ **①** From Shamley Green pond follow the road at the edge of the green towards the main road. Turn L on the side road to the footpath between gardens (100m). Follow it around bends to the field (200m) then up beside the hedge (150m).

② Turn R on the path across the top of the field (Greensand Way). After the church cross the road into the church car park (450m).

ⓔ *Extension of 2 km/1¼ mile: Turn L on the path near the road*

(150m). In the large field diverge R aiming for the nearest trees behind the highest point. Follow the edge to the track in the trees (450m).

ⓕ *Turn R (50m). Pass L of the house to the field (250m) and cross ½R to the bridge (100m). Go out along the track (300m). At the L bend aim for the house (20m) then turn along the L bank of the canal (200m). Cross the road and canal to the Run Common layby.* ✿

ⓖ *From the layby follow the path L of the road (200m). Turn R under* *the first bridge. Keep on along the course of the Horsham Railway under the 2nd bridge (550m) to the 3rd bridge (600m). After it climb the path L to the farm track.* ➔④

③ Stay ahead (GW) between fields, over a farm track (300m) down to a tarmac drive (400m). ✧ Slightly R, find the onward path and continue down to the rivulet (200m). Cross and follow the R edge to the top of the field (150m). At the track continue ahead over the old railway bridge (100m).

④ Walk down through Rooks Hill Farm to the main road (300m).

⑤ Go along the broad verge near the hedge (150m) and cross to the track beside the house, GW. Keep on between the fields up past the garden hedge and down the drive to the road (450m). ★

⑥ Take the footpath up the bank, opposite, through the trees and up the L edge of the field (300m). After the wood at the top, continue in the same line down to the gate in the valley, and up the field R of the farm house to the track (200m). Go round the bend and up the track to the trees (100m). ✿ (Look back at the Wey valley, 1½ miles wide.)

⑦ At the L bend, turn R up the bridleway in the trees. Keep on to the tarmac drive at the house, Daneshill (400m). ❀

⑧ Go R down the drive to the T-junction (300m) then L down past Birtley House (nursing home) to the main road (600m).

⑨ Cross to the pavement and turn L. Follow the road round the curve and up the rise (300m). Just before the top take the track R down under the bridge (with Downs Link path on the route of the Horsham Railway), over the Junction Canal and the Bramley Wey (200m).

⑩ Don't turn L with the track but climb to the fields and go straight over to the next road (550m).

⑪ Go R on the road (50m), round the L bend and on all the way to Shamley Green (800m).

Trig points give joy to walkers and status to hills. They were built for the third triangulation of Great Britain which the Ordnance Survey initiated in 1936 and became redundant in 1990 when global positioning technology was thought as accurate as traditional survey methods. In all, about 6500 were built. The English ones are mostly tapered square pillars of local stone or concrete. The fundamental mark is a brass stud set in a concrete block a metre below the pillar and there is another in the bottom of the pillar. The brass spider on top is for fixing instruments.

In triangulation, angles from two points, accurately sighted on a third, allow its position to be calculated by trigonometry, hence trigonometric survey and trig point. Sightings were made at night using lamps. In the 1950s trig points were painted white for aerial surveying.

Gibbet Hill (Hindhead) trig point (1938) was used in the primary triangulation over distances of 50km/30 miles. Hydon's Ball trig point (1952) was secondary with triangles of 8km/5 miles. The first triangulation started in 1784 from a base line which now ends in Heathrow.

Ordnance Survey - map makers to Britain since 1791 T Owen & E Pilbeam OS 1992

38 Grafham and Wintershall

About 8 km/5 miles with extensions of 1 km/¾ mile and ¾ km/½ mile; undulating farmland and woods on the Lower Greensand; bluebells in season.
OS maps 1:25000 145 +134, 1:50000 186 Aldershot.

Start from Rushett Common, TQ 022 423; park in one of the rough laybys on the minor road near the A281 junction.

Linking walks   29✦   30◉
32❖   37◇   39◉   40✳

From the layby follow the minor road away away from the A281 past the houses and pond L. ◉

(e) *Extension of 1 km/¾ mile: After the pond (100m) take the 2nd track L (200m). Just over the* Horsham Railway *bridge, corkscrew down L under it on the Downs Link path. Stay ahead (SE) on the DL under a road (500m) to the next cross path 100m after a cart track L (450m).*

(f) *Turn R through the trees and keep on along the L edge of the field to the end (400m). Turn L to the Whipley Manor drive (20m) and follow it R up through Whipley Manor Farm (450m) ✳ to the main road, A281 (100m).*

(g) *Cross to the side road opposite and follow it past Goose Green Farmhouse R (350m).* ✦④

① After the pond (250m) turn R on the footpath into the end of the first field, opposite the track from the farm. Follow the L edge to the far

76

end (400m) and go on between gardens to the main road (100m).

② Go L along the pavement past Grafham Church and on up the slope (300m).

③ At the top cross to the drives and take the L one (70m). Go past the house into the field and follow the edge R round to the wood (150m). Go on through the trees (100m) then ½R down the next field to the R edge where it curves away R (200m). Transfer to the field R. Cross the L end into the trees (50m) and follow the track to the road in front of Goose Green Farmhouse (150m). ✳ Turn R.

④ Before the next house R watch out for a path L across Goose Green (100m). Follow it into the field (100m). Cross to the hedge bend and keep on L of the hedge (100m), over the footbridge and up the R edge of the next field to the tarmac drive of Tilsey Farm (300m).

⑤ Turn R. Stay ahead past the pond L, between barns then on the gravel track R of a hedge and down to the bend at the trees (700m).

⑥ Keep to the main track round the pond past the house (100m). Stay ahead on the minor track in the scrub. When it bends L (80m) enter the field R and go straight up, aiming for the middle of the top edge (200m). Pass through the gap into the next field then L up to the adjacent field (30m). Follow the R edge out to Nore Lane, the track between fields (150m). ❖ ⬂

ⓧ *Extension of ¾ km/½ mile: Turn L up the sunken track (130m). At the bend climb the stepped path R. Turn R and follow the edge of the field up onto the ridge (700m).*

ⓨ *At the top turn R on the horse track up the ridge between fields (Gatwick Airport distant R) (150m). Keep on into the wood, down to the oblique cross track (400m).* ❸

ⓩ *Turn R then stay ahead down to the road (400m). Go down the road R (40m) and join the footpath on the other side.* ➜⑨

⑦ Follow the track R over the rise and down to the road (700m).

⑧ Walk up the road L over the ridge and down past Scotsland Farm (300m) to the footpath R 40m before the R bend (50m). ❸

⑨ Follow the path (GW) round R below the hillside field at the edge of the wood then L into the field (500m). Go on across the field parallel with the top edge (200m).

⑩ Take the track out at the other side over the little valley but when it bends R stay ahead steeply to cross another track (150m) then over the grass past the corner of the Wintershall gardens down to the boundary track before the cottage (200m). Continue along the track which curves R to Gatestreet Farm (450m). ✦❖

⑪ Turn R along the road (150m) and L at the next junction down past the next house (350m).

⑫ Turn R, beside the house, on the path to the fields (100m). Stay ahead at the L edge then from stile to stile (200m) and down the middle of the long field (usually no visible path). Pass close to the bulges in the wood R to the gate at the bottom edge, 50m from the R corner (400m). Go out ahead (150m) to the main road and cross the corner of the Common to your parking place.

39 Shamley Green and Whipley

About 10 km/6¼ miles with an extension of 2 km/1¼ miles; undulating farmland.

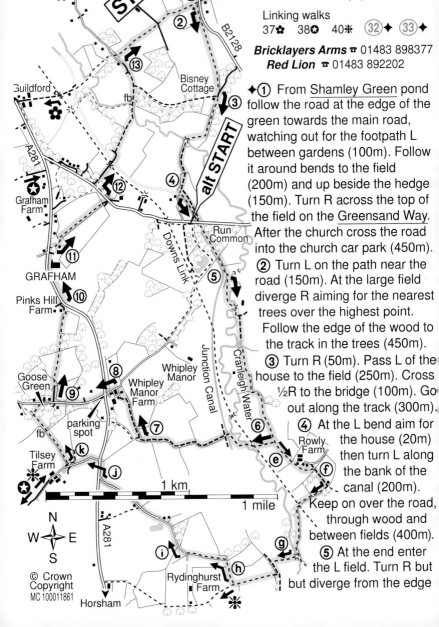

OS maps 1:25000 145 Guildford + 134 Crawley, 1:50000 186 Aldershot.

Start from Shamley Green, parking at the roadside in Woodhill Lane near the pond, TQ 032 438, or from Run Common layby, TQ 032 419.

Linking walks
37✿ 38✪ 40✳ �32✦ �33✦

Bricklayers Arms ☎ 01483 898377
Red Lion ☎ 01483 892202

✦① From Shamley Green pond follow the road at the edge of the green towards the main road, watching out for the footpath L between gardens (100m). Follow it around bends to the field (200m) and up beside the hedge (150m). Turn R across the top of the field on the Greensand Way. After the church cross the road into the church car park (450m).

② Turn L on the path near the road (150m). At the large field diverge R aiming for the nearest trees over the highest point. Follow the edge of the wood to the track in the trees (450m).

③ Turn R (50m). Pass L of the house to the field (250m). Cross ½R to the bridge (100m). Go out along the track (300m).

④ At the L bend aim for the house (20m) then turn L along the bank of the canal (200m). Keep on over the road, through wood and between fields (400m).

⑤ At the end enter the L field. Turn R but but diverge from the edge

© Crown Copyright
MC 100011861

down to Cranleigh Water. Follow the bank round towards E Whipley farmhouse. Cross the cart bridge to the gate R (40m). Above, follow the track R along the valleyside fields (200m). At the concrete part go round the bend then R as before (200m). In the next field go up the L hedge (100m), then on as before to the side path down R, 200m before Rowly Farm (250m).

ⓔ *Extension of 2 km1¼ miles: Stay ahead up to Rowley Farm. Pass between the houses and gardens then go round the L edge of the field (350m) and R along the track to the next house (150m).*

ⓕ *Enter the field R and go down the L edges (200m). Cross the Downs Link path and carry on round L to the footbridge R (350m).*

ⓖ *Cross the stream and go on between fields (200m) then L on the track (100m). At the junction go R on the track then path to the end of the long field R (300m). ✳*

ⓗ *Turn R on the side path (150m). When it ends in a field, follow the hedge L to the farm drive (300m).*

ⓘ *Walk along the drive R to the next houses (350m) and on along the lane to the main road (500m).*

ⓙ *Turn R on the road R (100m) and L up the Tilsey Farm drive (250m). Stop inside the gateway. ✪*

ⓚ *R of this gateway, level with it, is a hedge. Go down the R side of it to the stream (300m) ahead over the next field (100m) and across Goose Green obliquely R to the road (50m). Turn R (100m). ➜ⓞ*

⑥ Turn R down to the bottom of the field. Cross the Downs Link path (150m) then the stream (100m) and continue R through

the valley and over the Junction Canal to the farm tracks (100m). Keep on up the track ahead at the L edge of the fields (600m).

⑦ At the top, follow the bend in the track towards Whipley Manor Farm and pass between the buildings to the main drive (450m).

⑧ Walk out of the farm L and cross the main road (100m). Carry on along the road opposite (350m).

⑨ Take the track R of Goose Green Farm into the field (100m) and go up the R edge (50m). Cross into the field R and aim obliquely for the middle of the top edge (150m). Go out through the wood (100m) and along the L edge of the next field past the house (150m). Join the drive L and walk down to the road (70m). Cross.

⑩ Follow the road L to Grafham Church (200m) and on (100m).

⑪ Just after the Grange drive L turn R on the narrow path under trees to the field (100m). Follow the R edge to the far end (400m).

⑫ Go L on the road (150m) and turn along the next track R over the Horsham Railway bridge (200m) ✿ to the next field. When the track bends L carry on near the edge ahead, straight on down to the stream (400m) and along the bank (100m). Cross the footbridge. Keep on up the path and along the track to the house (300m).

⑬ Continue on the tarmac drive (70m) then take the side path R up between the fields all the way to the church car park (650m).

⑭ Cross the main road. Turn L along the edge of the churchyard and carry on beside the road into Shamley Green (300m).

40 Whipley and Smithbrook

About 8¾ km/5½ miles with extensions of 1¼ km/¾ mile and 400m/¼ miles and (if starting from Smithbrook Kilns) a short cut of 2½ km/1½ miles; undulating farmland. OS maps 1:25000 145 Guildford+134 Crawley 1:50000 186 Aldershot.

There is no large parking place except at Smithbrook Kilns. Start from the verge outside Whipley Manor Farm, TQ 026 408, or the side road opposite.

Linking walks 32✳ 34✤ 38✳ 39✳   **Smithbrook Kilns cafe**   01483 276780

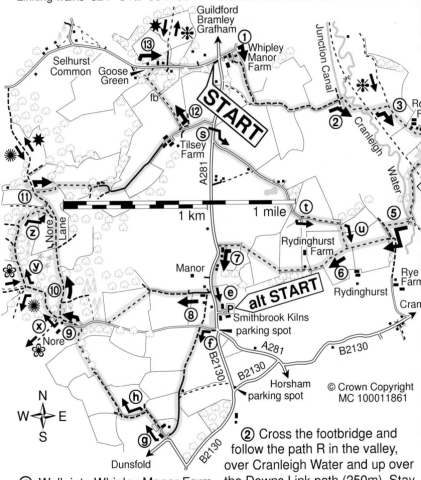

① Walk into Whipley Manor Farm from the A281 (100m) and turn R between the house and barn. Stay ahead on the track which bends L then follow the L hedge (450m). Carry on round the L bend down through the fields (R of hedge at first) to the Junction Canal (600m).

② Cross the footbridge and follow the path R in the valley, over Cranleigh Water and up over the Downs Link path (250m). Stay ahead up the field (150m).

③ At the top turn R on the South Wey path to Rowly Farm (200m). Pass between the houses and gardens then follow the edge round L (200m). Turn R on the track to the next house (150m).

④ Enter the field R and go down the L edges (200m). Cross the Downs Link path and carry on round L to the footbridge R (350m).

⑤ Cross Craneigh Water and go on between fields (200m). Turn L to the path junction (100m) then R on the track. Stay ahead between fields, past a side path R (300m).

⑥ Keep on round the top edge of the next field, L of the farmhouse (350m) and on beside the wood (150m). In the next field cross ½R to the exit 100m from the far R corner (250m) then follow the line of stiles/gates to the A281 (150m).

⑦ Follow the road L (300m).

ⓔ *Extension of 1¼ km/¾ mile in summer: Keep on beside the road past Smithbrook Kilns to the next road junction (200m).*

ⓕ *Just before it, turn R up the drive (100m). After the first field take the track L between the fields to Painshill Farm (800m).*

ⓖ *Before the road, turn back R up the tarmac drive between barns and continue on the track (200m).*

ⓗ *Before it curves round the end of the field R take the side track L over the rise and down until it splits to the fields (200m). Turn R on the track up the R edge and go on up the top field. Watch out for the path out R under the trees. Follow it to the lane (700m). Turn L.* ➔⑨

⑧ Turn R on the track at the drive of Manor Cottage. Carry on at the R edge of the fields to the entrance to the top field (400m) then ½L up the middle of the field to the top L corner. The path is often invisible (350m). At the lane go up the slope R past the Pheasantry drive to the gateway of Nore (200m).

⑨ Fork R up the rough track to the track junction (100m). ✳

ⓧ *Hilly extension of 400m with fine views: Turn L & R and carry on steeply up the hill to the path junction on the ridge (400m).*

ⓨ *Fork up R then keep to tracks on the R edge of the ridge (450m).*

ⓩ *Carry on off the end, down R (300m). Near the bottom go L (50m) then down the stepped path R to the track and L (150m).* ➔⑪

⑩ Don't go round the bend but stay ahead through the wood, past a side track R from the fields (500m) and over another rise to the dip with the pond (sometimes dry in summer) (450m). ✳

⑪ 20m before the pond, turn R through the field, R of the hedge (180m). At the corner, drop to the adjacent field L (30m) and turn into the adjacent field R. Cross slightly R to the protruding corner of the wood before the house (200m). In the trees turn L to the house (80m). Go on round the pond (100m) and L up the main track. Stay ahead through Tilsey Farm along the drive to the gateway 80m after the barns and just after the pond R (700m).

ⓢⓣⓤ *Cut of 2½ km/1½ miles back to Smithbrook (only on map).*

⑫ Level with the gateway is a hedge L between fields. Get to the R side of that hedge and follow it down to the stream (300m). Keep on over the footbridge to the hedge bend then cross the field slightly L to the stile (100m). After the trees bear R across Goose Green to the road near houses (50m). ✳

⑬ Walk along the road R to the A281 opposite Whipley Manor Farm (400m).

The **A3** is the London to Portsmouth road of ancient importance. The old road from London Bridge passed through Kingston, Guildford, Godalming and other towns which were successively bypassed. The Hindhead bypass took the form of a 1830m tunnel under Gibbet Hill which opened in 2011.

Albury was the Domesday Book manor ELDEBERIE. It already had a church and mill. The estate stayed in the d'Abernon family for 5 centuries but has passed through many families since. The medieval village was near the old church but in the 18th century pressure was put on villagers to move to the present site and Henry Drummond, a 19th century owner, built the new village church in 1842. Notable residents have been Malthus the political economist, Anthony Devis the painter and Martin Tupper the writer. The estate came to the Dukes of Northumberland through the marriage of Drummond's daughter.

Albury - a short guide to the parish 1998 24pp

Barnett Hill, the house, was built about 1905 in Queen Anne style by a London businessman, Frank Cook. His widow gave it to the Red Cross in 1944. It had already been used as a convalescent hospital and became the national training centre and archive. It is now a conference centre.

Binscombe has several old houses and the air of an ancient settlement. The area was one of the ancient tithings of Godalming. The housing developments which have joined it to Farncombe have brought to light much broken pottery of the Roman period. *Bin* may derive from bean or from a personal name.

Blackheath was the name of the Domesday Book hundred that included Bramley, Chilworth, Shalford, etc. The men of the hundred would probably have met and held courts in the open on the heath. The village lies in the midst of the Common, 108 hectares, managed by Waverley BC for recreation and conservation. The Canadian army enclosed it as a camp in World War II which ended the grazing; it had been used for army training for the Napoleonic wars and in Victorian times. It had a pub originally called *The Volunteer Arms*.

Bramley was a great Saxon estate of 34 hides. It probably included Dunsfold, Hascombe, Alfold and Cranleigh, for the Domesday Book lists no other place between BRVNLEI and the Sussex border and it had three churches and five mills. William the Conqueror awarded it to his half brother Odo, the Bishop of Bayeux. Bramley Mill is a 17th century building which operated until 1935. A railway platform is retained with fervour despite the absence of rails and trains. The church, Holy Trinity, is probably on the site of one of the Domesday Book churches but the nave is Victorian. The aisles are almost as large as the nave. The oldest fabric extant is the west door arch (inside the porch) which is probably Norman. The chancel dates from around 1210.

Bramley & Grafham - a short history Bramley Village Society 1977 47pp

Catteshall Manor house was the headquarters of the Pitman organisation 1952-96. It appears to be a large Victorian house but has a 17th century core and remnants of the structure of Henry I's time. He detached Catteshall from the large royal manor of Godalming for his retainer Dyvus Purcell. The timber-framed house at the bottom of the hill (sometime The Ram pub), is ancient, originally a hall house ie with a central roof-high room containing a hearth but no chimney. The pub took its name from the hydraulic ram (in the roadside cavern) installed in the 1920s by John Blake Ltd to raise water to Unsted Park.

Catteshall Mill was one of the three Godalming Domesday Book mills. In 1141 it was part of a grant to Reading Abbey. Its earliest recorded uses were as a fulling mill and a corn mill. The rent in 1509 was 43 shillings and 10 sticks of eels! By 1661 it was a paper mill and in 1885 one of the first to use wood pulp. A sales poster of 1906 says it produced 80 tons of paper per week. In 1869 the wheels were replaced with a turbine which last rotated in 1960. This was the largest known Fournyron turbine (37 kW); there is a model of it in Godalming museum. *Catteshall Mill* Alan & Glenys Crocker *Surrey Arch Soc Research Vol 8* 1981 64pp

Chantries Hill is a Greensand ridge with thin seams of Bargate stone which give greater fertility and permit grassland instead of heath in the Five Fields. It was given to Holy Trinity Church, Guildford in 1486 by Henry Norbrigge (mayor, d.1512; there is a brass plate to him near George Abbott's tomb). The rent or produce of a chantry paid a church for prayers for the soul of the donor or others. Usually it funded a church school whose pupils chanted the prayers. Chantries were dissolved soon after the monasteries by Acts of 1545 & 1547.

Chiddingfold is a nuclear village with church, inn and pond clustered at the corner of the green and the old houses round it. *The Crown* may be the oldest inn in England deriving from a Cistercian rest house of 1285. The first reference to the present site is in 1383. Edward VI visited and his retinue camped on the green in 1552. Despite its evident antiquity Chiddingfold is not in the Domesday Book, its tax being lumped with Godalming's at that time. The earliest mention is of Chedelingefelt in a charter of about 1130. It became a market town in 1300 by charter of Edward I when it was the main centre of glass production and within the great iron making area. About 40 glassworks sites have been identified locally, ten in the parish. Ancient church accounts elsewhere show orders for Chiddingfold glass. The village church, St Mary, has lancet windows, pillars and chancel arch in Early English style dating from soon after 1200. The nave roof was raised around 1450 on extended pillars. The lych gate with its coffin table and Horsham slab roof was added in 1888 and restored in 1980. *Chiddingfold - the village and history of the Parish Church of St Mary* H R H White 1999 44pp

Chilworth is CELEORDE in the Domesday Book, a small manor with a mill, owned by Bishop Odo of Bayeux. The present manor house is a 17th century re-build by Vincent Randyll, owner of manor and gunpowder mills, 1653-73, who sold up to the Duchess of Marlborough after the South Sea Bubble.

Chinthurst Hill was bought by Surrey County Council as public open space in 1961 to forestall building. The tower is a folly built in 1936 when the Chinthurst estate was part of Lord Inchcape's property. An ancient boundary mound on the hill is close to the modern Waverley/Guildford border. The eponymous house, 1895, was Lutyen's first large commission. It is now subdivided.

Compton is ancient. There was a Roman house but the name first appears in writing in 727 when 4 hides of Compton were gifted to Chertsey Abbey. It is CONTONE in the Domesday Book, a manor of 14 hides owned by Edward the Confessor and tenanted by Brixi. In King John's time it was split into the Manors of Down (north of the Hog's Back), Polsted, Westbury, Eastbury and Field Place, still represented by large houses of these names. The *Harrow Inn* has been licensed since at least 1780. White Hart Cottage is a 15th century house; it was a pub (before 1780) and may have been the church ale house. *The History of Compton in Surrey* Lady C Boston Compton Parochial Council 1987 247pp

Compton Church, St Nicholas, has a Saxon tower. The nave walls were replaced by hard chalk pillars when the aisles were added about 1160. The Norman doorway (inside the porch), font, lozenge mural over the chancel arch and coloured glass in the east window are all 12th century work. The chapel above the sanctuary is very unusual and its wooden guard rail exceedingly old. A Crusader graffito is scratched on the south side of the chancel arch.

Cosford Mill has the oldest machinery in Surrey and parts of the building are 15th century. It closed in the 1890s. The wheel was removed for iron in WWII.

Cranleigh Water is a small river in an immense valley which provides fine views from its sides, the hills above Shamley Green and Hascombe. It is aligned with the Guildford notch in the North Downs so must be regarded as the original River Wey though it is smaller than the present major tributaries.

Cutt Mill is mentioned in a medieval document in 1273 when it was given in a marriage settlement by John le Cotte to John le Paumer. The mill functioned until the 1930s but the only remains of it are the pillars and shed in front of the house. The present house is the mill cottage. The millpond would be medieval in origin but the Tarn and the ladder of ponds a mile up the valley are Repton's work of the 1800s when he landscaped Hampton Park.

The Devil's Punch Bowl first appears in name in Rocque's Map of the County of Surrey of 1765. Its old name was Highcombe or Haccombe or, in a charter of 909, Hegcumbe which may derive from hay-growing where the bottom has cut down to the Atherfield Clay. From inside it appears to be surrounded by hills but it is a very large coomb set in the side of one - Gibbet Hill. The clay raises the water table into the sides. The several springs easily sap the Hythe beds which are mainly unlithified sands but the sides remain steep because of low rainfall and the sand causes absorption rather than run-off.

Dunsfold was Duntesfold when first heard of in a 1241 assize roll. It became an industrial parish in 1568 when a forge opened. Later owners were Richard Wyatt of Shackleford and Lord Montague. *Fold*, Saxon *falod*, implies a place of sheep folding. *Dunt* is a Saxon personal name. Folds held sheep in winter; in spring shepherds would have led them off along moltways to wander on the heaths. The area has the greatest concentration of *fold* names in Britain,

Dunsfold Church, St Mary & All the Saints, is almost in its original form of around 1260-1320 when Early English was becoming Decorated. In Victorian times the chancel arch was raised, the east window truncated and the west window rebuilt. Points of interest: the cruciform plan unusual for a small village church, very ancient pews, three plug holes for floor washing visible externally (one in the west wall) and the elaborate sedilia.

Dunsfold airfield assembled jet fighters until 2001. It was constructed in 20 weeks by Canadian Army Engineers in 1942 as a Royal Canadian Air Force base in the build up to D-Day. It started with Mustangs, which shot up trains in France, and went on to have Mitchell bombers. After the war in 1946 it was loaned to Skyways Ltd whose Skymasters and Dakotas made 2749 flights in the Berlin Airlift (1948-49). Hawker took over in 1951, for testing prototypes and assembling the Sea Hawk, Hunter, Folland Gnat, Hawk and Harrier. In recent times the televison series *Top Gear* has been made there.

Dunsfold, Surrey's most secret airfield Paul McCue 1992 Air Research Publications 297pp

Eashing is listed as Æscengum in Alfred the Great's will drafted around 885 - a bequest to his nephew Ædhelm. It is Escingum in the Burhal Hidage written about 915. This was crown land and approximately equidistant from London, Winchester and the sea. Lower Eashing was a farming hamlet. Tankards, built about 1700, was perhaps a farm manager's house. The block of offices, half on the island, replaced Eashing Mill in 1998. This mill may have been one of the three Godalming Domesday Book mills. It was sold as a corn mill in 1658 but converted to paper making in the 1830s. By 1865 its 98 employees made 10 tons of paper per week for The Times and other newspapers. Latterly it was a flock mill then became an engineering works. The 13th century Eashing bridges are of Bargate Sandstone and similar to the Wey bridges at Tilford, Waverley, Elstead and Unsted, generally attributed to the monks of Waverley.

Elstead would have been in existence at the time of the Domesday Book but it is not listed because its data was lumped in with the rest of the great manor of Farnham. The name is first documented in the founding charter of Waverley Abbey in 1128 when two acres of HELESTED were donated by the Bishop of Winchester. The old houses of the village are the 16th century Peace Haven and Lilac Cottage in Milford Road, Old Farmhouse in Farnham Road and Domford in Thursley Road. The forge at the green dates from 1686. Polshott Manor was the Stovold family farmhouse for 400 years from the 15th century but has not been a working farm since 1920. Brookside started as a small 16th century cottage but has grown. Peter Sellers (1959) and Ringo Starr lived there. Elstead Bridge was re-built in the 16th century and resembles the bridges attributed to the Waverley monks. The second lane was added during World War II.   *Elstead then and now* Gillian Drew 2001 81pp

Elstead Church, St James   , was a chapel of Farnham by 1291 but building styles suggests it was started in the middle of the 12th century. Built of chalk and bargate, the 14th century parts still visible are the blocked doorway in the chancel, the pointed chancel arch and the middle window in the north wall.

Elstead Mill still has its wheel but is a restaurant. The building dates from about 1800 but is likely to be on the site of one of the six Domesday Book mills of Farnham. When work ceased in 1881 it was making worsted fringes. In the 17th century it had been a corn, malt and fulling mill and the previous building was erected in 1648. Helstede mill was entered at 10s 3d in a rent roll of 1208.

Enton was part of the Rectory manor of Godalming owned by Flambard. He was the chief adviser of William Rufus but lost his land when the fatal arrow brought brother Henry to power. Enton Mill survives incorporated into a house. It probably originated in the 15th century; milling ceased in 1899.

The **Ford Farm** fish ponds are used for producing trout to stock angling ponds on the Albury estate and at Syon House - for the same owner.

Gatwick is a fairly common name from the Saxon for goat place or farm. This would be consistent with the surrounding heath.

Gibbet Hill is the second highest hill in Surrey, the trig point at 272.85m/895'. The Celtic cross is for the murdered sailor. The lane skirting the northern edge of the hilltop follows the line of the old Portsmouth road with the sailor's stone 100m down W where the body was found in 1786. The subsequent A3 was cut into the hillside below but dug up in 2011 when replaced in the tunnel.

Godalming Hundred appears as a bequest in the will of Alfred the Great, drafted around 885. The charter for a market was given by Edward I in 1300. Borough status was granted by Elizabeth I in 1574 and held until 1974 when the town was subsumed into the Borough of Waverley. The coat-of-arms has a woolsack: Godalming was a centre for sheep rearing, weaving, fulling and dyeing, in medieval times, with power provided by the Rivers Wey and Ock. High Street was the London to Portsmouth road with several coaching inns. The *Kings Arms* still looks like a coaching inn; Peter the Great stayed there in 1698. The *Red Lion*'s public bar was the old Godalming Grammar School. Prisoners on the way to Portsmouth for transportation were incarcerated at this inn. The Pepperpot is the old Townhall. It replaced the medieval Hundred House (court and office) on the same site in 1814. The town was a terminus on the LSWR branch line from Woking in 1849 but the present station opened in 1859 when the railway was extended to Havant, connecting with Portsmouth.

Godalming - a Short History John Janaway 1993 Ammonite Books 77pp

Godalming Church, SS Peter & Paul, was restored by Gilbert Scott in 1879. It is a well preserved large medieval church built on the original Saxon walls with some 9th century carved stones. The lead sheathed spire is 14th century.

The **Godalming Navigation** reached Godalming in 1763, extending the Wey Navigation from Guildford. It consists of stretches of improved river bed and cuts, rising 10m/32 feet from Guildford with locks at Millmead, St Catherine's, Unsted and Catteshall. Freight was carried until 1925 when the wharfs closed. In 1968 the commissioners gave it to Guildford Corporation who off-loaded it to the National Trust. *London's Lost Route to the Sea* P A L Vine David & Charles 1973 267pp

Gosden Common was the venue for a cricket match reported in the *Reading Mercury* in 1745 which appears to be the first known women's match; plaque on the pavilion. The Bramley maidens scored 119 notches and the Hambleton maidens, 127; lbw may have been a problem. Gosden House, now a school was Osbert Sitwell's grandmother's and appears to appear in his work.

Grafham comes to light as an estate sold by Waverley Abbey around 1238. A much later owner was Henry Woodyer, the architect, who built the church, St Andrews, in 1864 when the parish was created out of Bramley and Dunsfold.

The **Greensand Way**, officially opened in 1980, is a 110 mile path from Haslemere, Surrey to Hamstreet, Kent.

Greyfriars Vineyard has open days. It started as a 1½ acre plot in 1989 on south facing Chalk, growing Chardonnay and Pinot Noir grapes. From 2011 the vineyard expanded and concentrated on the production of sparking wines.

Hambledon is HAMELDONE in the Domesday Book. No church was recorded then but tax documents show there was a church by 1291. The present church was erected in 1846 but has memorials from earlier churches. Court Farm, the 17th century house next door, was the Manor House which held Courts Leet and Courts Baron. The kiln opposite the church was for chalk lime for making mortar. The *Merry Harriers* is an 18th century house.

Hambledon Hurst has fine forest oaks on Wealden Clay. It typifies the terrain which gave the Weald its name, Saxon for forest, and which made penetration of the country difficult before hard roads were built. The toll road, now the A283, was built 1780-90 and raised in 1820. The toll booth is beside the road.

Hammer ponds powered mills that worked the hammers, bellows and lathes for furnaces, foundries and forges. Thursley had three hammer mills, two beside the Common. Lower Hammer Pond remains; the site of Upper Hammer Pond is crossed by the A3. The earliest record is a lease from the Mores of Loseley in 1625 and pig iron was still arriving for forging in 1767. There is no evidence of smelting; the Wealden iron industry was in its final phase when work spread into Surrey and no slag has been found. Lower Hammer Mill was converted to a silk mill for which there are records early in the 19th century.

Hascombe is not a Domesday Book manor but appears to have been detached from Bramley around 1300. Hascombe Place Farm (17th century) was the manor house. At the village fountain local people still bottle their own free mineral water. The church, St Peter, is Victorian Gothic, built of Bargate in 1864, incorporating memorials, font and screen from the previous churches. The painting of the chancel is unusual. The advowson goes back to 1305.

Hascombe Hill or Hascombe High Beech, 624ft/190m, has an Iron Age fort on top. During the Napoleonic Wars, it had an admiralty shutter signalling station.

Heaths in England occur in a low rainfall arc from Dorset round to East Anglia in places where soils are well drained and deficient in calcium. However they are man-made in origin. The vegetation would have started as oak woodland whose leaf-fall and animals caused a soil rich in humus. The sandy soils were easy to dig and plough for the first farmers in the Neolithic period. Removal of the trees and depletion of the nutrients by crops would quickly have produced badland. It could be used by shepherds but the browsing of sheep and goats as well as rabbits and deer removed tree seedings and prevented regeneration of woodland. Pre-1950 photographs show much Surrey heath without trees but the absence of sheep and goats and the introduction of myxomatosis allowed the encroachment by birch and pine. Now only heath preservation prevents the return to oak wood. Dust and animals would very slowly re-supply the calcium.

 The heaths are very different from the wheat fields and grassland of the North Downs Chalk and the land on the calcareous Bargate sandstone. In a rich soil the grains of sand, silt or clay are coated in humus, a gel. This sticks the grains together, spaced out with air between them and holds all the water, nutrients and useful bacteria. In heaths, the angular sand grains are spaced with more than 60% air, good for plant growth, but lack calcium. Calcium is a plant nutrient and influences soil structure. Without it the humus does not gel so water and nutrients are not retained and the acidity is not neutralized. Sand rivers in the footpaths show the lack of adhesion.

The plants that thrive are species that 'dislike' calcium (calcifuges), heathers, bilberry and bracken and those that withstand dryness like gorse and broom. Hilltops are most drained, south facing slopes most heated, gravel soils least retentive. Snails are absent, no calcium for shells, but insects abound. Reptiles are thought to be favoured by the dry soil which warms up quickly in spring and lengthens the insect year. In wet heath, water fills the air spaces and mire plants thrive, like cotton grass, bog asphodel and *Sphagnum* mosses. Lack of oxygen prevents decay so dead plants accumulate and form peat.

The **Herpetological** Conservation Trust owns several areas of heath on Witley and Hankley Commons. Bare patches and piles of logs are made for basking.

Hindhead grew up on the boundaries of Thursley and Haslemere parishes and Frensham in Hampshire, solely to serve the London to Portsmouth Road. In the middle of the 19th century there was an inn, *The Royal Huts*, and three cottages. Conan Doyle built the house Undershaw. The Devil's Punchbowl Hotel was built as a country house by the Hon Rollo Russell, son of Lord John.

The **Hog's Back** is the part of the North Downs where the bending of the strata is most extreme - the bedding in one of the chalk pits has a dip of 60°. The name first appears in a letter of 1802 quoted by Mowbray Howard in The Longs of Jamaica and Hampton Lodge. Gilbert White was still calling it Guildown in his diary in 1797. The road on top may be the oldest in England.

The **Horsham Railway** line from Guildford, opened in 1865 and closed in 1965. It began the demise of the Wey Navigation and Junction Canal and suffered the axe of the Dr Beeching cuts in 1965. It is now the route of the Downs Link path which goes under or over the bridges.

Hurtmore is HORMERA in the Domesday Book, a manor rated at 15 hides. It had been owned by Edward the Confessor but, after the conquest, went to Walter, Son of Othere. Local place names include *priory* because, from 1259 until the Dissolution, the manor belonged to Newark Prior (near Woking); it was leased to farmers for income. *Hurts* is or was local vernacular for billberries.

Hydon's Ball is a curious name for a hill. Perhaps it had a signalling station with a ball. It is an outlier of Folkstone sands on Bargate beds so has heath on top and fields below. The trig point is at 178.82m/587'. The reservoir in the hilltop receives water from Greensand boreholes and serves Chiddingfold, Dunsfold and Hambledon. To the west, Blackdown is the distant, asymmetric hill, the highest in Sussex. The knobbly peak to the right is Gibbet Hill above Hindhead. On the opposite side the North Downs are visible. The granite seat marks the gift of the land to the National Trust as a memorial to Octavia Hill.

The **Junction Canal** linked the thriving Arun and Wey Navigations in 1816. Much of it is now dry and some of it has been filled in. It was conceived at the time of the Napoleonic Wars and promoted as a way of avoiding French privateers on the sea route between London and Portsmouth. The Arun Navigation reached Newbridge in 1787. The Wey Navigation reached Guildford in 1653. Both had been successful but the Junction Canal across the Weald came too late and leaked. It paid for itself but proved a poor investment for the owners. The peak trading year for all three was 1839. There are moves to restore it.   *The Wey and Arun Junction Canal* P A L Vine 1999 Tempus 128pp

King Edwards School, Witley, originated in the same charter of Edward VI as St Thomas' Hospital and Christ's Hospital in 1553. It started in Bridewell Palace where Katherine of Aragon had lived and which the boy king gave the City of London at the suggestion of Bishop Ridley. The aim was to provide destitute youngsters with artisan skills, replacing the social services of the monasteries and chantries, recently dissolved. After a period in Southwark the school moved to new buildings in Witley in 1867. The buildings were requisitioned for the Royal Navy in WWII for the development of radar.
King Edwards School Bertie Mawer Ian Allan 2000 144pp

Ladywell Convent is the mother house of the Franciscan Missionaries of the Divine Motherhood, a nursing order. The house was built in 1911 as the family home of Major General Douglas Scott, Tuesley Court. It became Ladywell Convent in 1956, as HQ, international postulancy and novitiate, when many buildings were added and the nuns moved from their Guildford nursing home. The order de-centralised in 1979 and now has branches in many countries.

Lammas Land was common land for growing hay but on which cattle could be grazed from Lammas, 1st August, to Candlemas, 2nd February.

The **Lion's Mouth** is a cleft in a raised Ice Age river bed on Hankley Common, presumably named and caused by the soldiers and their vehicles over the last hundred years. 100m west is the Atlantic Wall built in WWII for practice attacks. Hankley Common is designated for parachute drops amongst its training roles.

The ridge top is thin gravel mainly of grey Hythe Sand-stone from the Hindhead area. Periglacial melts of the Weald ice cap would have cut rivers into the soft sands leaving gravel on the river bed. Afterwards, ½m years of low rainfall erosion lowered the land except where protected by the gravel which now causes the ridge. This is a "fossil" tributary of the River Blackwater which ran through London before the Thames joined it. The remnants of it still flow from Aldershot to the Thames.

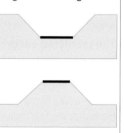

Littleton was a Domesday Book manor, LITELTONE, held by Wulfwy Hunter before and after the conquest; presumably he was the king's hunter. Most of the old cottages in the village are 17th century: 8 & 9, 22 & 23, Pillar Box Cottage, Long Meadow, Littleton Farm & Willowmede.

Loseley House is open to visitors on summer afternoons. Loseley icecream used to be made here. Loseley was the Domesday Book LOSELE. The estate has been the home of the More (now More-Molyneux) family since the 16th century. Sir Christopher, Treasury Secretary to Henry VII bought the estate in 1508. His son, Sir William, an adviser to Elizabeth I, built the present house in the 1560s using Waverley Abbey stone after the dissolution. The muniment room yielded 2240 documents from Tudor times and earlier, letters, court rolls, etc. As the Mores were lords of other manors round about these are a useful source for historians. Marrying the 17-year old Ann More in 1601 without her father's permission brought John Donne a year in prison which occasioned his epigram "John Donne, Ann Donne, undone", to which we might add "well done" as they went on to produce at least ten children! *Donne* and *done* rhymed.

Lynchets are steps in ground level, indicative of ancient farming. Ploughing on slopes promotes soil creep down to hedges and away from them below. If the hedges are removed, steps remain. Lynchets occur in woods and towns.

Milford Hospital pioneered tuberculosis treatment. It started as Surrey County Sanatorium in 1928. TB sufferers stayed three years or more to isolate them and give them the best living conditions to fight the bacterium. The 110 acres were worked by the patients for occupation, training and finance. Galton and Simpson met and wrote their early sitcom scripts there in 1948 when they were TB patients. After Thoracic Surgery moved to the Royal Surrey Hospital in Guildford it became a Rehabilitation Hospital for the Elderly in 1980.

Minepit Copse would have received its name when the Weald was the chief medieval region of iron making. Siderite (iron carbonate) mudstone nodules dug from the Weald Clay were the richest ore, up to 75% iron by weight. The shallow mines were always back-filled. The woods were intensively managed by coppicing to provide the charcoal for smelting and forging. A 1570 court roll of the Loseley Papers has the commoners in dispute with Lord Montague for taking too much wood for his ironworks which was in Dunsfold parish.

The **Moat** pond on Thursley common is absent from maps until the early OS editions so it may have been dug mid 19th century, possibly as a duck pond.

Monks' Hatch, now the name of a house, would have been one of the ways to the farm when the Cistercians of Waverley Abbey owned Wanborough. Its farmland stretched over the Hog's Back. The heavy-looking bargate bridge was by Lutyens for the Compton bypass of 1931, ornamented by crosses where it crosses the Pilgrim's Way. The new bridge for the A3 opened in 1989.

The **murdered sailor**'s name is unknown. Walking to Portsmouth in 1786 he fell in with three travellers at Godalming. As they had no money he agreed to fund them on the journey. They were last seen together in the *Red Lion* at Thursley. His body was found at the spot marked by a stone on Gibbet Hill; Dickens has Nicholas Nickleby reading the inscription to Smike as they walk to Portsmouth. The sailor's grave is in Thursley churchyard. The ruffians were arrested in Rake, trying to sell his belongings. They were hanged in 1787 at Kennington Common and hung in chains on the gibbet on the hill, their bodies tarred for preservation. The Celtic Cross memorial was set up in 1851 on the command of Lord Chief Justice Earle on the site of the gibbet when it fell.
POST OBITUM SALUS After death, salvation IN OBITU PAX In death, peace
POST TENEBRAS LUX After darkness, light   IN LUCE SPES In light, hope

Baring Gould's Hardy-esque novel, The Broom-squire, tells of the life of the sailor's fictional daughter around Thursley and the Devil's Punch Bowl.

The **North Downs Way** is a modern concoction for walkers designated by the Countryside Commission in 1978. It runs 131 miles from Farnham to Dover mainly following ancient drove roads which are likely to be some of the oldest trade routes in England.

Oakhurst Cottage, Hambledon (National Trust 01428 684090) is open to the public some afternoons and can be visited by arrangement. It is a 16th house, furnished as a 19th century labourer's dwelling.

Octavia Hill, 1838-1912, was a co-founder of the National Trust. She was the offspring of reformer parents and the NT was the outcome of the idealism and philanthropy stirred up by industrialization and urbanization. The founders met through participation in the Commons Preservation Society (to oppose illegal encroachment) and the Kyrle Society (to improve urban areas by planting). Robert Hunter drafted the constitution and legislation, Hardwicke Rawnsley had the contacts from his many campaigns and Octavia Hill was the indefatigable workhorse. Their ultimate solution was to own places worthy of preservation and the National Trust for Places of Historic Interest or Natural Beauty was registered under the Companies Act in 1895. Most social reforms of the age became the welfare state but the NT continues more or less as it started. It now controls more than ½m acres, 230 houses and 130 gardens.

Park House, the manor house of Peper Harow, was built in the Italian style in the 1770's to the designs of Sir William Chambers. The 350 acre grounds were laid out by Capability Brown. The cedars in the fields were planted from pots in 1735. The cricket field was the scene of one of the earliest recorded cricket matches in 1727. The estate was the seat of the Brodrick family (Viscounts Midleton), from 1713 to 1943 when two sons were killed in action. The house was used by the Canadian Army in WWII, then became a special school and is now apartments. The finest building is the stable block, now a residence.

Peper Harow's boundary appears in a charter of 909. It was PIPERHERGE in the Domesday Book, a manor rated for 5 hides. The most likely derivation of the name is *Pippa*, an Anglo-Saxon personal name plus *hearg*, a heathen temple. The present estate village has cottages, big house, church, farm and pond all in a cluster. Home Farm, Pevsner considers the best assemblage of farm buildings in Surrey, with its granary on wooden piers. The dovecote in the field was built in 1763; the dovecote at the farmyard entrance, in 1775. The church, St Nicholas, is first mentioned in a tax document of 1291. It is medieval in style but was rebuilt by Pugin in 1847. The tower had been added in 1826. Points of interest: the 1487 brass (near altar) for Joan Adderley; the memorial and grave of Sir Henry Dalrymple who led the charge of the Heavy Brigade at Balaclava; the stone about a stone in the chancel floor

The **Phillips Memorial** in Godalming was for Jack Phillips, the radio operator of the Titanic which sank in 1912. The cloisters were designed by Hugh Thackeray and the garden by Gertrude Jekyll.

The **pillbox**es are World War II relics of the GHQ line which stretched from the Medway to near Gloucester to defend London and the Midlands. The line follows natural obstacles such as the Downs, canals and rivers.

Pillboxes - a study of UK defences 1940 Henry Wills Secker & Warburg 1985 98pp

Polsted Manor was created before 1160 by sub-division of the large Saxon manor of Compton. The present house is relatively modern. The gardener's cottage has Tudor features and may be part of the original manor house.

Postford and Waterloo Ponds appear in a map of 1660 and the lane runs along their dam which would have been built for the earliest gunpowder mills. Postford Mill (called Albury Mill when demolished in 1996) was built in 1809 to make paper which it did until 1875. After this it made furniture fabric then animal feed. Finally it became a trout farm. Another Postford Mill, 100m upstream, owned by the same family was the one which made bank note paper execrated in Cobbett's *Rural Rides*. He contrasted Chilworth's beauty with its industries: *two of the most damnable purposes namely the making of gunpowder and banknotes. Paper Mills of the Tillingbourne* A Crocker Tabard 1988 77pp

Prior's Field is an independent, trust school for 300 girls, 11-18. Founded by Julia Huxley, mother of Aldous, and grand daughter of Arnold of Rugby, the main building was by Charles Voysey of the Arts & Crafts Movement.

Puttenham Common is worth exploring but very disorientating. It belongs to the Hampton Estate but is managed by SCC for recreation and conservation. An Iron Age fort, Hillbury, stands on the hilltop overlooking Hampton. Roman bricks and tiles have been found nearby and numerous Stone Age tools. Lascombe, at the eastern edge, is a Lutyens house.

Puttenham village lies in an area with evidence of population from mesolithic times. The Domesday Book lists most villages round about but not Puttenham. It does state that Wanborough had formerly been two manors. The first documentary mention of Puttenham is from 1199. The medieval village had three fields under strip cultivation and the South Field probably gave its name to Suffield Lane. The Pilgrims' Way went through the village and there used to be a pilgrims' fair in December. The oldest houses are the 15th century timber-framed Rosemary Cottage, Old Cottage and Winter's Farm. The brick houses, Hook Lane Farm, Street Farm and Farm Cottage date from 1520-50.

Puttenham under the Hog's Back Ruth Dugmore Phillimore 1987 247pp

Puttenham Church, St John The Baptist, is Norman in origin, the south wall of the nave dating from about 1100 and the pillars from about 1160. The tower was added about 1400 but lost its spire to fire in 1735. The window between the porch and the tower is the re-used early 14th century east window. There is a brass of 1481, a memorial for Edward Cranford, Rector. An ancient well in the churchyard came to light Palm Sunday 1972 when a tree disappeared!

Puttenham Priory is a 17th century brick house with a Palladian façade added by Thomas Park in the 18th century. It was never part of a monastery but the manor was willed to Newark Priory (near Woking) by Philippa de Melville in 1248. The priory would have drawn income from the profits of the land and an earlier house may have been occupied by its steward. In modern times the house has been a hospital and a business headquarters.

Rodsall Manor was probably the Domesday Book REDESSOLHAM, held in 1066 by the Saxon thegn, Tovi. In recent times a local historian has measured the field areas to show they accord with the Norman assessment of 5 hides. The present house was built in 1680 and two rooms were added in 1724.

St John's Seminary was built in 1890 for training priests for the Roman Catholic diocese of Southwark. It now acts as the regional seminary and takes overseas trainees. The red brick building is in the Jacobean Dutch style.

St Martha's Hill is a Greensand hill. The soft sands contain seams of Bargate sandstone which hold the hill together and form steps in the steep paths. The top is hardened by ironstone of which the church is built and over which the path passes east of the churchyard. Just south of the church a reservoir for Chilworth is sunk in the hill. Several round houses have been excavated here.

St Martha's Church is of Saxon origin but the oldest walls (the transepts) date from about 1087 and the chancel from about 1250. It was largely rebuilt in 1848. The hill seems to have been called Martyrs' Hill in Saxon times and the name may derive from this. During the 13th - 16th centuries the church was under Newark Abbey, the priest's house being below at Tyting Farm. By the east gate is a memorial stone to Yvonne Arnaud, the actress.

Shackleford was a tithing of Godalming. It has some of the best examples of bargate houses galetted with ironstone chips. The bargate Victorian Gothic church at Norney, St Mary, is by Sir Gilbert Scott in 13th century style.

Shalford was SHALDEFOR in the Domesday Book. One of the families to hold the estate in modern times was the Godwin-Austins of K2 fame. The Church, St Mary's, is Victorian but replaced an earlier building of 1789. There were medieval and Saxon churches before that.

Shalford Mill, on the Tilling Bourne, still has its working parts intact and is open on certain days weekly. There was a mill on the site in 1332 but the present structure is 17th century. It was acquired for conservation by "Ferguson's Gang" in 1931 and now belongs to the National Trust.

Shamley Green is best seen when cricket is in progress; some of the roads are within the field of play and cottages are protected by nets. It appears in Verse 5 of the *Just So* stories and somewhat earlier in a tax list of 1332 which had a Thomas ate Shamele, when it would have been a hamlet of Wonersh. Notables of the parish have been T S Eliot, W O Bentley (cars), Alfred Hitchcock and Harry Secombe. The church, Christ Church, was consecrated in 1864 as a chapel of Wonersh. The reredos and east wall are elaborately painted.

Shamley Green - a history of the village Shamley Green History Society 1993 61pp

Snowdenham Hall was built in 1886 as a country mansion for Robert Courage the brewer. It is now apartments.

Somerset Bridge is a corruption of the name of an early ford, *Sumeræs forda*, listed in 909 as a boundary mark for Farnham in a charter of King Edgar.

Street House was the home of the London family that produced Sir Edwin Landseer Luytens, the architect, 1869-1944. His first job at 19 was to adapt the Thursley village shop and his early works were within reach of Thursley by bicycle. He completed 550 commissions: houses, memorials, cemeteries, palaces and bridges. The Surrey houses were succeeded by work all over the world: the British Embassy Washington, the Viceroy's residence New Delhi, the British Pavilion at the 1900 Paris Exhibition and the London Cenotaph.

Lutyens and the Edwardians Jane Brown Penguin 1997

Thorncombe Street has the air of an ancient settlement. The name first appears as Torncumba in 1205 when Stephen de Turnham acquired the estate. Beatrice Lilley aka Lady Peel owned the estate in the 1930s.

Thursley has a pre-Christan name derived from Thor's clearing, presumably a place of worship. It is not in the Domesday Book, being then part of Witley Manor, but the Saxon church indicates it already had a population. The village lies on the old London-Portsmouth road with several picturesque old cottages near the church. Hill Farm, next to the churchyard, has soot on the rafters indicating the old part was a hall house, perhaps 14th century, and Wild Goose Cottage has a jutting upper storey unfashionable by 1550.

Thursley Church, St Michael & All Angels, has a massive oak frame inserted around 1500 to support the bell turret. Points of interest: Saxon windows and wafer oven in the north wall of the chancel, a Saxon window in the nave; Saxon font; sundial on the turret; several 18th century table tombs; the graves of the underlined murdered sailor (facing the war memorial) and John Freeman the poet.

Thursley Common is a National Nature Reserve of English Nature. It has the richest dragonfly fauna in Britain and all the British reptiles. Uncommon birds nest here: Dartford warbler, hobby, nightjar, stonechat, snipe, curlew and reed bunting. As well as dry heath there is mire with the irregular holes of old peat diggings. The Cricklestone and Thor's Stone are ancient boundary marks, Thor's probably aquiring its romantic name from *The Broom-squire*. The long mound with the board walks is on the Saxon boundary of AD 688, when the Wessex king, Cædwalla, gave the Farnham lands to the Bishop of Winchester.

The **Tilling** Bourne is a major tributary of the River Wey. It runs for about 20 km/13 miles between the Chalk and Greensand ridges fed by springs from both and joins the Wey at Shalford waterworks. It powered up to 30 mills and was a major industrial valley in Britain from medieval times until coal-fired industry started. It now has trout farms and watercress beds. *Bourn(e)* is gognate with *burn* (from Anglo Saxon) so *Tillingbourne River* is tautological.

Tuesley was TIWESLE in the Domesday Book. Tiw was a Saxon god. This area has a great concentration of pre-Christian Saxon names in England (Wanborough, Thursley, Peper Harow, etc). The first influx of Saxons seems to have come across the Weald from the coast of Kent and Sussex and according to Bede the Kingdom of Sussex was the last to be Christianised.

Tuesley Minster is thought to be the 2nd church listed in the Domesday Book entry for Godalming and is probably 7th century. It existed long before the parish system and would have been the religious centre for the whole district. Excavated in 1860, the building had a nave of 21' x 14' and a room with nine skeletons. Pope Gregory advised St Augustine to put churches on the sites of existing temples, so it is likely that Tiw was worshipped here.

Unsted Park is a rehabilitation hospital and school. The Adam-style house was built in 1750 by John Sparkes and the stables were added in 1874. It was a hospital in WWI and the National Provincial Bank training centre 1949-72.

Unsted Manor is a half-timbered house just off the route, built in the 14th & 16th centuries but not a true manor house. The name first appears in 1256 as Tunchamstede when the land was acquired by William de Wintershull.

Unsted Bridge is the lowest of the 13th century bridges attributed to the monks of Waverley, like those at Eashing and Tilford. It crosses only a backwater now, the River Wey having moved across the valley.

Wanborough was the Saxon manor WENEBERGE of the Domesday Book. Its Lord, Leofwin, according to tradition, was killed at the battle of Hastings. A few days later it was laid waste by the Norman army skirting London prior to the English capitulation. It was bought for £100 in 1130 as a grange for the new Waverley Abbey whose lay-brothers would have worked it, hence the local place names with monk or greyfriars. It gave its name to Wanborough Illinois when Morris Birkbeck, the tenant farmer, emigrated to America in 1817 with workers from Wanborough and Puttenham. St Bartholomew's was a Saxon church re-built in the 12th century with defensive strength.

Wanborough from White Barrow to World War Gillian Drew 1993 28pp

Wanborough Manor house was the farm house of the one-farm manor. It bears the date 1527 when it still belonged to Waverley Abbey but architectural detail suggests it was built 1650-70. In World War II it was the SOE (Special Operations Executive) training centre for resistance organisers for France and it flits through the espionage novels of Ted Allbeury. Trainees were not allowed to speak English and local people called them *the foreigners*.

Wanborough Great Barn is Surrey's most important medieval aisled barn. Guildford Museum arranges open days and group visits. 1388 is the building date suggested by tree ring data but the octagonal pillars were cut early in that century, presumably for an earlier building. The barn was in agricultural use until about 1988 and was fully restored in 1997. It was not a tithe barn.

Watts Chapel in the cemetery is remarkable. Financed by Watts and designed by his wife Mary (d 1938) it is in Italian Romanesque style with symbolism based on the Circle of Eternity and the Cross of Faith. The decorative bricks and gesso panels were made at the terracotta works by 74 villagers.

The Word in the Pattern Mrs Watts Astolat 1904/Watts Chapel Veronica Franklyn Gould

Watts Gallery displays 500 works of the painter and sculptor, George Watts. Art treasures from the London galleries were stored here in WWII. Until 1956 the adjacent buildings were a studio and factory for terracotta ware, using the underlying Gault clay. A Roman house excavated in 1914 in the Watts' garden at the nearby Limnerlease yielded three coins dated from 313 to 378. George Frederick Watts (1817-1904) sold 5 shilling portraits at the age of 16 and served as House Artist to the British Ambassador in Florence. His best known bronze is the equestrian *Physical Energy* in Kensington Gardens. He was a friend of Dickens, Thackeray and Tennyson. His first wife was Ellen Terry.

The **Wealden Clay** gives problems to walkers, farmers and builders. It is not a soil but a layer more than 1000' thick most of which is unlithified (unsolidified). It formed 125m years ago, before and thus below the Greensand and Chalk but is exposed in the middle of the Weald. The name is misleading because it includes strata that are not clay but hard rocks such as Horsham Sandstone used for roofing slabs and various Sussex marbles used for church memorials.

Where the substratum is clay, the soil is a clay soil. Tiny particles grip water so it is easily water-logged, denying air to roots. Cereals are grown where slopes aid drainage but elsewhere it has wood or pasture. The streams cut little ravines called *gills* or *ghylls*. The gills, clay and forest made cultivation and travel difficult so the Weald was thinly populated until hard roads and bridges arrived. Oaks were taken for ship building and there was much coppicing to make charcoal for iron working. Siderite nodules out of the clay made this the main iron producing area in Roman times and the Middle Ages. In more recent centuries the clay has been used for brick-making which still continues.

Westbrook House in Godalming is a Jacobean house with Georgian additions owned by The Meath, a charitable home and centre for epileptics. General James Oglethorpe (1696-1785), inherited it and lived there. He was an MP for Haslemere, a general of ambivalent affinities in the army that put down the Jacobite rebellion and the founder of the American colony of Georgia (1732).

Westbrook Mill is probably on the site of one of the Domesday Book mills. Westbrokesmyll appears in the leet records of 1483. In 1881 when it was a leather works it generated for the first electric town lighting anywhere.

The Brilliant Ray Francis Haverton Godalming Centenary Celebration Committee 1981 18pp

The **wetlands** near Unsted are watermeadows of the Wey which have snipe, teal, shoveller ducks, dab chicks and water rails, easy to see in winter.

Winkworth Arboretum (National Trust) started as a private venture. Wilfred Fox (1875-1962) a London doctor living nearby bought 95 acres in 1937 which he planted with temperate maples, Azaleas, Liquidambars and Sorbus species. He gave a 62 acre site to the NT in 1952 and 35 acres more in 1957.

Wintershall was a manor cut off from the great Manor of Bramley around 1227, aka Selhurst. In 1723 it was bought by the Barretts (of Wimpole Street). In recent years it has been the venue for a summer passion play.

Witley is WITLEI in the Domesday Book, a large manor rated for 20 hides with a church. There were no other estates before Sussex. Ancient variants of the name rarely have *h* so the likely derivation is *Witta's* not *white* clearing. The waste of the ancient manor became Hindhead, Thursley and Witley Commons. The malmsied Duke of Clarence was one of the medieval owners. George Eliot (née Mary Ann Evans 1819-1880) lived at Witley Heights from 1876 until shortly before she died and wrote her last novel, *Threophrastus Such*, there.
The History of Witley, Milford and the surrounding Area Elizabeth Forster 1999 Witley P C 83pp

Witley Church, All Saints, has a Norman doorway inside the Victorian porch but most of the nave wall is late Saxon, 1½ windows surviving from that time. The wall paintings are 12th century. The style of the chancel, transepts and tower is Early English and a 12th century roof survives in the south transept. Like most ancient churches the windows have been enlarged in later styles.

Witley Park is a private house and the manor house of Witley. It used to be Lea Park. In modern times it has been owned by a succession of industrialists but was emparked in the original sense (for deer) in 1247. The 3-mile Bargate wall was built in the 1890s. Lord Pirrie, a Belfast ship builder, owner in the 1900s, was the cause of P in the old iron gates of the estate.

Wonersh has splendid old houses suggesting ancient settlement. It is not in the Domesday Book, however, probably then being part of the large manor of Bramley. The Pepper Pot in the road junction is a modern village folly originally conceived as a bus shelter. On the green is a Victorian reading room built for the Gosden tannery workers. The *Grantley Arms* is a genuine old house with olde worlde additions. It was the *Hector Inn* in 1687. It was used in the first Dick Turpin (silent) film in 1912. Woodyers is a 17th century house improved in the 18th. Green Place is a Georgian house with a 16th century wing and has internal work back to the 14th century. The jettied, timber framed Old House in the main street dates from about 1600; the middle section was jacked higher in 1979 to prevent flooding. In the gate house to the field beside the churchyard see the high frieze in low relief modelled on villagers in 1953. The church, St John the Baptist, is largely 18th & 19th century but the oldest fabric may be part of one of the Domesday Book churches of Bramley. Points of interest: the arch between the tower and nave of around 1180; several brasses.
Wonersh - a Guide to its Principal Buildings Wonersh History Society 1996 44pp

Wonersh Mill is now a store shed on the other side of the mill pond from the house. A map of 1679 shows a corn mill here. The mill house dates from the 15th century but has had many additions. Milling ceased in 1910.

Wormley has no records ancient enough to allow interpretation of its name but snake clearing would seem appropriate. It is a hamlet of Witley enlarged by Coopers' factory which made walking sticks from coppiced wood and the school, King Edward's. The wartime Naval presence led to the establishment of the Institute of Oceanographic Sciences in 1952 which developed sonar for the mapping of the oceans but moved to Southampton in 1995.

The **Wyatt Almshouses** were built about 1622 funded by £500 in the will of Richard Wyatt, 1554-1619, who lived at Hall Place (now gone) in Shackleford. He owned the Dunsfold foundry and had other irons in the fire, eg a wharf in London. He was elected Master of the Carpenters' Company of London.